演讲的艺术
课堂活动教师手册

The Art of
Public Speaking
Activities for the English Public
Speaking Classroom

Stephen E. Lucas (美)　　顾问

田朝霞　周红兵　　编著

外语教学与研究出版社
FOREIGN LANGUAGE TEACHING AND RESEARCH PRESS
北京 BEIJING

参编人员（按姓氏拼音排序）

陈志红	华中师范大学
丁　洁	洛阳师范学院
郭　建	中国科学院大学
黄　珊	华东交通大学
刘　瑛	吉首大学
陆小丽	湖北大学
聂　薇	北京外国语大学
时丽娜	复旦大学
万　玲	首都医科大学
汪希平	皖西学院
肖　琪	文华学院

前言及编写说明

英语演讲教学在中国的发展可能超出不少人的想象。2005年，斯蒂文·E.卢卡斯（Stephen E. Lucas）教授受邀来到中国，首次在全国举办英语演讲教师研修班。当时，绝大部分英语教师只知道演讲比赛，不知道"演讲"还是一门课程。回顾起来，这次研修班应当是将遵循西方传统的"公众演讲"课程大规模地引进中国高校的标志了。仅仅10年的发展，全国已从屈指可数的几所高校在"英语口语"名下开设演讲课，发展到目前已有几百所高校开设。期间，卢卡斯教授多次在中国举办英语演讲教师研修班，传授教学理论与方法，奠定了国内英语演讲教学的基本模式。外研社引进和改编的《演讲的艺术》第十版（中国版）也成为首选教材。

在几次全国演讲教学与研究学术研讨会以及教师研修班上，不少教师提出，希望有一本课堂活动手册来指导演讲课堂的设计与组织。据卢卡斯教授介绍，美国定期出版名为 *Selections from the Speech Communication Teacher* 的教师手册，是以真实的课堂教学实践为基础的教学方法总结，其核心理念是"Written by classroom teachers for classroom teachers"。这正是教师们所需要的。于是，这本《演讲的艺术课堂活动教师手册》（以下简称"手册"）便诞生了。手册的策划和编写由卢卡斯教授全程指导，众多一线教师参与。它旨在构建有效的演讲课堂，并为英语演讲教师提供展示与分享的平台。

主要特色

这本手册具有以下几个特色：

实用性。手册直观地展示课堂活动过程，详细描述活动的具体操作步骤以及时间分配，大部分活动还配有示范性的教学材料，如PPT课件、视频等*。活动描述在语言上力求简洁、清晰，一目了然。可以说，每一项活动都像是在演示一堂示范课。教师可以直接将活动搬上课堂，也可以灵活使用。

参与性。手册的编写理念是"Written by classroom teachers for classroom teachers"。

---

* 本书的相关PPT课件、视频等教学材料请登录高等英语教学网（heep. unipus. cn）下载，进入网站后，请点击"教材支持中心"，在"英语专项技能"—"演讲类"栏目中下载相关材料。

活动的原始材料均来自中国和美国高校的一线教师，由众多国内教师参与编写。他们不仅分享活动设计，还分享教学体会。这本手册是集体智慧的结晶。

开创性。类似的课堂活动手册在高校英语教学出版物中还较为少见，该活动手册具有一定的开创性。特别值得一提的是，许多活动设计都充分考虑了"翻转课堂"的理念，将"课堂活动"置于高校语言类课堂教学的中心位置。这些尝试是对网络时代新的教学模式的探索。

基本结构

全书框架。全书分为三大章。第一章（Teaching Procedures—General）为一般的课堂教学过程，包括导入、课堂讨论、反馈等环节。第二、三章直接针对演讲。第二章（Preparation and Presentation—General）为纵向线索，话题贯穿演讲准备及呈现的整个过程，包括选题、制订提纲、写作、演讲表达等环节；第三章（Speeches of Specific Types）为横向线索，涵盖几类常见的具体演讲类型。

单元结构。每个单元分为三个部分。"Understanding Teaching"包含 2–3 句与教学或本章话题相关的箴言警句，从宏观上启发教学；"Teacher's Guide (Q & A)"对单元话题的知识体系和重要的教学环节（尤其是教学难点及解决方式）进行梳理；"Activities"针对具体问题，介绍 2–3 项课堂活动。

使用说明与建议

《演讲的艺术课堂活动教师手册》主要配合《演讲的艺术》第十版（中国版）教材，供教师设计和组织课堂教学使用，也可以用于一般的"英语演讲"课堂，大部分章节还可应用于其他语言类和部分修辞学类课程的教学设计。活动广泛涉及英语演讲的理论与实践话题，活动风格体现了多样性，可以满足演讲课教师的不同需求。

配合教材使用。本书可作为教师上课时随身携带的"手册"，原则上不能代替教材，尤其在知识体系的介绍上，仅点到为止，详解论述仍需参考教材。

融入"翻转课堂"。这里需要说明三点。第一，解决英语演讲课上"理论"与"实践"的冲突。本手册中大部分活动的设计采纳"翻转课堂"的理念，即学生课下学习理论知识，教师课上引导、协助并检查学生的演讲实践。"Pre-Class Reading Assignment"提示学生提前阅读相关知识点。第二，正确理解活动范例的涵盖范围。与话题对应的每个单元均包含 2–3 项活动设计，但这些活动只涵盖了一部分知识点。换言之，这些活动主要帮助教师设计课堂组织形式，而知识体系则需要参考

"Teacher's Guide (Q & A)"，并督促学生课下完成阅读。这部分自学的内容，学生可以自己阅读教材，也可以借助外研社开发的《演讲的艺术》数字课程。最后，翻转课堂必须重视学生课下任务的完成情况以及教师的反馈，这里不赘述。

重视"评论／反思"。"Comments/Reflections"部分对活动进行解释和补充，特别对活动的适用情境以及灵活操作进行说明。

行文语言的处理建议。该手册采用以中文行文为主，辅以英文行文的方式。知识体系及活动过程描述均采用中文行文，目的在于方便教师阅读和参照。一般仅需 10 分钟左右便可对一项活动过程了如指掌，"In-Class Procedure"部分完全可以作为课堂活动操作的参照。英文行文的部分主要是教师上课可能用到的内容，如指令、反馈等。

　　本手册的第 1–5、7–9、17、18 单元由周红兵老师整理编写，第 6、10–16、19–21 单元由田朝霞老师整理编写。特别感谢卢卡斯教授提供的美国课堂活动相关资料以及全程指导，感谢各位国内供稿老师的慷慨分享，感谢外研社郑建萍、陈静等诸位编辑的辛勤劳动。其中各种不足与不周之处，恳请各位同行批评指正。也衷心希望各位老师有更多参与，盼望手册第二辑的早日推出。

田朝霞
2015 年 1 月于南京

Contents
目 录

PART

1

Teaching Procedures—General

Warm Up

UNDERSTANDING TEACHING

A good beginning is half done.

—A Proverb

A single spark can start a prairie fire.

—Unknown author

TEACHER'S GUIDE (Q & A)

➤ **Warm Up对一堂课有何重要性?**

演讲课是一门需要学生积极参与、抒发观点的课程。教师需要不断鼓励学生开口,通过设置适合他们的课堂活动,使学生释放外语学习焦虑而引起的紧张情绪,更好地参与到演讲课的教学活动中来。减缓学生的紧张,最有效的途径之一就是上课开始时的 Warm Up 活动。

- Warm Up 的活动设计以简单为宜。例如,在讲授信息性演讲一节时,教师可先提出几个基本问题,如 What's your favorite food? Why do you like it? What do you need to prepare before you make it? 这些问题只需学生按照实情作答即可。因此,学生也不会特别紧张。这将有助于他们开口说英语,找到信心,也会更主动地参与到接下来的课堂教学与活动中。

- Warm Up 是一堂课的开端,良好的开端是成功的一半。那么,如何在上课开始的三至五分钟吸引学生的注意力,激发学生的求知欲? 怎样把新旧知识有机地结合起来? 这些对于上好一堂课都十分重要。

- Warm Up 还可以有效地帮助学生进行课堂语境的切换。高校的学习环境决定了学生经常需要在短时间内从一个教室切换到另一个教室,从一门课程切换到另一门课程。一个精心设计的 Warm Up 对帮助学生进行这种语境切换有积极的作用。

➤ **Warm Up 活动设计有哪些基本方法?**

- 承上启下,温故知新。"温故而知新",由旧知识引入新知识,这符合学生循序渐进的认知规律。运用此原则导入新课,关键在于找出新旧知识的内在联系,即它们的结合点。通过精心的语言组织,使 Warm Up 活动成为新旧知识的连接点,自然过渡到新课的主题。

- 设置疑问，开启思维。思维从疑问开始，所谓"多疑善问，增长才智"。因此，提出问题，设置疑问也是一种很好的课堂导入方式。探求"为什么"的好奇心和求知欲，是激发学生主动学习、深入探讨的动力。根据学生的心理特点和教学内容，提出耐人寻味的问题，或设置悬念，诱导学生跟进。
- 巧引故事，活跃气氛。在课堂上巧妙运用各种故事或逸闻轶事，不仅可以活跃课堂气氛，而且可以培养学生对课程的浓厚兴趣，同时还可以开拓思维，帮助记忆。
- 巧设悬念，引起注意。在新课的开始，提出与新知识密切相关的新颖有趣的问题，紧紧抓住学生的心理，吸引学生的注意力。

➤ 该教学环节何时进行?

- Warm Up 适用于所有的课堂教学，无论是第一次课还是最后一次课，是教师主讲的课堂还是以同学示范或课堂演讲为主的课堂，授课教师都有必要在核心内容的教学之前安排一至两个 Warm Up 活动。
- Warm Up, 顾名思义，是正式授课前的热身活动。一般情况下，教师提前准备好内容，学生即兴作答。少数情况下，教师根据实际情况临时调整活动的细节内容。

➤ Warm Up 活动应注意哪些方面的问题?

- Warm Up 的时间不宜过长，以一堂 45 分钟的课为例，一般不宜超过 10 分钟。
- 活动环节不宜过于复杂。活动设计需要考虑以下几点：指令和规则应简洁易懂；活动需在预期时间完成，不影响主体教学；学生不致过于紧张疲劳。
- 活动类型不宜太多样，一堂课一到两个 Warm Up 即可。

➤ 常见的教学困难

- 学生配合度不高，甚至会导致活动搁浅。建议充分备课，并设计补充方案。
- 学生兴致高昂，教师不能按计划转入教学重点，影响教学任务的完成。建议教师注意引导，并严格控制活动时间。

➤ 教与学的误区

- 不重视 Warm Up 环节，甚至省略该环节。
- 简单地认为 Warm Up 就是提出几个与授课内容相关的问题。
- 活动仅针对少数学生，忽略活动的参与面。

1.1

A Drawing Speech of Introduction

Goal:	To allow students to get to know each other.
Class Size:	Any.
Time:	8–10 mins.
Pre-Class Reading Assignment:	Speaking in Public (*APS**, Chapter 1, pp. 2–15).
Materials/Preparation:	A. A number of questions for students to ask each other. The questions include name, major, interest, family, job, favorite things, hometown, etc.
	B. Some sheets of clean paper, some crayons and magic markers.

🕐 In-Class Procedure

PPT/Directions	活动过程描述
1–2 *Directions:* Now we're going to have some pair work on your personal information. Your task is to get the information of your partner by interviewing him or her. You can find your partner on your own.	1. 学生随机或就近挑选一个搭档，三到五秒钟内完成。 2. 学生需要用PPT上展示的问题访问自己的搭档，获得问题的信息和答案。
3. Questions for the Interview • Your partner's name • Your partner's major • Your partner's interest • Your partner's family • Your partner's favorite things • Your partner's personality …	3. 教师展示PPT幻灯片上的问题。学生可以挑选自己比较感兴趣的两到三个问题，没有必要全部都问。

（待续）

---

* 本书中，统一用 *APS* 代表《演讲的艺术》（*The Art of Public Speaking*）第十版（中国版）。

PPT/Directions	活动过程描述
4. Interview Round 1 • Two minutes. • Note down the responses.	4. 开始第一回合的访谈。提醒学生一定要记得自己所获得的有效信息。（两分钟。） 学生访谈时，教师可以在教室里面走动观察，同时注意控制时间。
5. Sort out your information. (one minute)	5. 当访谈时间达到两分钟的时候，教师立刻叫停。要求学生整理自己所获得的信息，时间为一分钟。
6. Interview Round 2	6. 第二回合的访谈。搭档不变，但学生的角色互换，即第一回合时的提问者，在第二回合中则为受访者。（两分钟。）
7. Sort out your information.	7. 教师控制时间，到时喊停。给学生一分钟时间整理信息。
8. • Choose interesting information. • Draw it out.	8. 给学生发放空白纸、彩色蜡笔、彩笔，要求思考并画出关于自己搭档最有趣的信息，注意是画出而不是写出。（两分钟。）
9. • Present your drawing. • Explain your drawing.	9. 选择一两位学生把自己的作品送给班上其他同学，受赠者将向全班展示作品。受赠者展示作品时，赠与者可解释作品的内容与意义。
10. Instructor's comments.	10. 教师在全班选取一两位同学进行评论，可以评论作品，也可以评论对作品的解释。

1. The drawings are often good conversation starters for both the instructor and students. When students are interviewing and drawing, the instructor will have the opportunity to meet the students and to know more about them.

2. As it is a warm-up activity, the time must be limited within 10 minutes. So the main task for the instructor is to monitor the time and to get students involved into the activity in an efficient way. Meanwhile, the instructor also needs to encourage students since some students don't feel at ease at the beginning of the class.

3. This activity is quite interesting, for some drawings are pretty funny, while some are quite elaborate and specific. So it will be helpful to get students involved into the activity. It will also be significant to reduce their nervousness at the beginning of the class.

本活动的设计源于以下文献: Bernum, Bia. (2004). A Drawing Speech of Introduction. In Lucas, Stephen E. (ed.) *Selections from the Speech Communication Teacher, 1999–2002*. Madison, Wisconsin: McGraw-Hill. 78–79.

Goal:	To create a "talk-friendly" environment on the first day of a performance course.
Class Size:	Any.
Time:	10–15 mins.
Pre-Class Reading Assignment:	Speaking in Public (*APS*, Chapter 1, pp. 2–15).
Materials/Preparation:	A. Compulsory questions: What are the names of the people in your group? What are their majors? Where are they from? B. Selective questions. The instructor selects some questions among the questions below, and the number of selective questions depends on the number of the groups in your class.

Selective Questions

1. Review the course description and objectives. What can your group expect to learn during this course? What does your group hope to learn?

2. Review the explanation of assignments. What questions and/or concerns does your group have about the assignments?

3. Review the general criteria for evaluating assignments. What questions and/or concerns does your group have about the criteria?

4. What is the attendance policy for this class? What should you do if you're late on a speech day?

5. What questions and/or concerns does your group have about the course policies?

6. What additional questions and/or concerns does your group have about the course, the course policies, and/or the instructor?

7. What is "academic integrity"? How does academic integrity relate to public speaking?

8. What are the general criteria for evaluating speeches? What questions and/or concerns does your group have about the criteria?

In-Class Procedure

PPT/Directions	活动过程描述
1–2 **Course Orientation** • Teaching plan; • Teaching objectives; • Grade & evaluation.	1. 首先教师利用15–20分钟的时间向学生介绍整个课程，包含课程的教学计划、教学目标、学生成绩评定以及课堂管理制度等。 2. 介绍完课程后，开始此部分活动。
3–4 *Directions:* The class will be divided into five groups. Each group will have five members. The last group could have four or six members. And each group will have to discuss two kinds of questions (one is compulsory to all groups and the other is selective). The group discussion time will be about eight minutes.	3. 把学生分成组，每组五人，最后一组则可以是四人或六人。 4. 每组将会需要讨论两类问题。一类问题是所有小组都要讨论的问题，另一类问题则每个组不一样，教师随机把小组与问题配对。
5. **Compulsory Questions** What are the names of the people in your group? What are their majors? Where are they from?	5. 教师在PPT上展示所有小组必须讨论的问题，见 Materials/Preparation A。
6. **Selective Questions**	6. 教师在PPT上展示可选择讨论的话题（参见 Materials/Preparation B），随机分配给各个小组。具体选择由教师自己决定，也可以小组自行选择，但各组讨论的话题不宜重复。
7–8 **Group Discussion** • Remember to take notes.	7. 教师宣布小组讨论开始，并且建议每组找一位同学进行记录，记下本组讨论的主要观点，以便最后在全班进行陈述。 8. 教师提醒小组讨论的时间为八分钟。
9–10 **Group Presentation Time!**	9. 教师选取一至两组的小组代表，向全班展示各自小组的讨论成果。 10. 最后教师进行简单讲评。

1. This activity is usually conducted on the first day of class. Students might be kind of silent at the beginning of the discussion. The instructor should introduce some information about the questions to students before the discussion. This will largely reduce students' nervousness and be helpful for them to break the ice when the discussion begins. When the instructor does the class orientation, please make sure students are focusing on the information provided.

2. The course syllabus and syllabus worksheets are then shown or distributed to students. The course syllabus includes the instructor, the course schedule, the course description, course objectives, course policies, brief explanation of course assignments, and general evaluation criteria.

3. This activity can be used in other English courses for group discussion.

本活动的设计来源于以下文献: Wood, Jennifer K. (2004). Using the Syllabus to Create a "Talk Friendly" Environment on the First Day of Class. In Lucas, Stephen E. (ed.) *Selections from the Speech Communication Teacher, 1999–2002*. Madison, Wisconsin: McGraw-Hill. 17–18.

Group Discussion

UNDERSTANDING TEACHING

The most fruitful and natural exercise of our mind, in my opinion, is discussion. I find it sweeter than any other action of our life.

—Michel de Montaigne

Freedom is hammered out on the anvil of discussion, dissent, and debate.

—Hubert H. Humphrey

TEACHER'S GUIDE (Q & A)

➤ **小组讨论有何重要性及意义?**

　　应用小组讨论的教学模式可以给课堂教学注入活力，它不仅可以使师生之间、学生之间更有效地进行交流，还可以培养学生的合作意识、团队精神，进而促使学生相互学习，共同提高，有力地促进课堂效率的提高。

- 小组讨论更能突出学生的主体地位，利于学生独立思考，培养主动参与的意识，激发学生的求知欲。

- 小组讨论能强化学生对自己学习的责任感和对同伴学习进展的关心。

- 小组讨论能为学生提供一个较为轻松、自主的学习环境，有助提高学生创新思维能力。小组讨论课堂教学中，师生之间、学生之间的交互活动是多边进行的，学生有更多的机会发表自己的看法，能充分利用自己的创造性思维，形成相同问题的不同答案，学习环境更为宽松，自主发挥的空间更为广阔。

➤ **该教学环节何时进行?**

- 小组讨论可以贯穿于所有的课堂教学，从演讲的基本要素到演讲类型的讲解；在课堂开始的 **Warm Up** 活动中，或是课堂最后一个要点的讲解中，都可以使用小组讨论的形式组织课堂活动。

- 小组讨论一般是指无教师主导的讨论。教师在讲解相关知识前，可以要求学生进行小组讨论，让学生在小组内，畅谈自己的看法，一句或几句话都可以。这样学生就会对相关知识有一个预热，在接下来的教师讲解时，学生会进行一些对比分析，这对促进学生进行批判性思维训练很有帮助。值得注意的是，小组讨论是在教师的各项指令安排下进行的，学生必须严格按照指令，积极参与小组讨论，作出自己最大的贡献。

> ### 小组汇报的形式及原则是怎样的?

- 小组汇报是基于小组讨论，由小组向全班进行的口头汇报，演讲者可以是小组的代表，也可以是小组的多位成员。小组汇报是小组讨论成果的最终形式，它既可以培养学生的演讲表达能力和创新意识，也可以促进学生的人际交往和团队合作能力。
- 小组汇报的展示方式可以多样，以使课堂更活泼、生动、有趣。小组汇报可由一位代表完成，也可由多位成员共同完成；可以采用陈述、对话、辩论、表演等多种方式。
- 各小组在进行汇报展示时，教师不应"袖手旁观"，应该认真听取各小组的汇报，并且记录详细的笔记，以给学生合理有效的反馈与建议。
- 小组汇报时，本组的非汇报成员以及其他各组成员都必须认真倾听，同时教师应该鼓励其他小组大胆质疑，也鼓励组内成员对已汇报同学的发言进行补充。

> ### 小组讨论活动应注意哪些方面的问题?

- 小组讨论的时间不能太长，以一堂45分钟的课为例，小组讨论活动的时间一般以20–25分钟为宜。时间太长，学生会无话可谈，偏离话题；时间太短，学生无法各抒己见，不能充分展示每个学生的想法。
- 在小组讨论活动中，有些学生始终保持沉默，好像活动与己无关。有的学生一开始有些害羞，可能只能说一两句话。为了防止出现这种情况，教师可以要求组员轮流担任小组长，来组织本组的讨论。
- 教师在进行小组讨论活动时，要加入到学生中，可以旁观，也可以直接加入某个小组，但不应是局外人。

> ### 常见的教学困难

- 组员之间不团结，不能形成合力。
- 学生对小组讨论话题的积极性不高。
- 每次汇报集中由一位同学完成，几次活动后便可能产生单调的感觉。

> ### 教与学的误区

- 教师认为小组讨论是学生的事情，成为一位旁观者。
- 教师经常挑选优秀的学生进行小组汇报。教师应关注和鼓励每一位学生。
- 所给的话题过于宽泛，未细化到容易操作的程度，以致讨论不能深入，不能达到预期效果。

2.1 Creative Problem Solving—From Top to Bottom

Goal: To introduce the three components of group problem solving: 1) clarifying and reframing the problem and goal, 2) brainstorming, and 3) establishing criteria.

Class Size: Any.

Time: 25–30 mins.

Pre-Class Reading Assignment: Selecting a Topic and a Purpose (*APS*, Chapter 4, pp. 44–57).

Materials/Preparation: 100 sheets of newspaper, five rolls of masking tape and a flexible ruler.

The classic stories of reframing the problem:

1. Early NASA engineers spent time and money trying to invent a new material to withstand the heat of atmospheric reentry. After failed attempts, someone at NASA realized that the goal was not to come up with a new heat resistant material but rather to protect astronauts from the heat of reentry. Reframing the problem quickly resulted in the ablation shield, made of simple graphite or porous ceramic which dispels heat as it melts and vaporizes away.

2. Experts like Champy (1995) contend that today successful organizations must constantly redefine their problems and goals to produce increasingly better solutions.

🕐 In-Class Procedure

PPT/Directions	活动过程描述
1–3 *Directions:* Each group will have 20 sheets of newspaper and a roll of masking tape. And each group will have five members to build a tower by using the newspaper and tape. Please try to build the tower as high as you can. The total time for this activity will be 20 minutes.	1. 教师向每组发大约20张报纸或废弃纸张，纸张大小一样；每组一卷胶带。 2. 每个小组包含五位成员（可以允许一组是四人或六人，视班上人数而定）。 3. 小组在正式制作前可以商讨具体方案，然后动手制作。全部时间为20分钟。

（待续）

PPT/Directions	活动过程描述
4. Explain the procedure to the whole class: Clarify Your Goal ↓	4. 教师向全班介绍整个流程。 · 首先各小组讨论，确定自己的小组目标，要制作多高的塔。 · 然后组员进行合作，用纸与胶带制作一座塔，塔越高越好。
5. Find the Criteria or Limitation ↓	5. 确定标准或分析困难。 小组在正式制作前可以商讨具体的方案，讨论在制作中可能碰到的问题，如何避免该问题。此部分讨论时间为三分钟。
6. Brainstorm Ideas for Building the Tower ↓	6. 小组头脑风暴来讨论如何制作纸塔。 教师鼓励学生在动手前进行小组讨论，要求每位组员给出自己的想法，最后小组形成一致意见。如果意见不能统一，可以采用举手投票的方式决定最后的想法。讨论时间为十分钟。
7. Select a Method After the Brainstorming ↓	7. 按照小组讨论的最后方法，开始实施方案，全组一起来制作纸塔。
8. Start to Build the Tower ↓	8. 开始动手制作纸塔。制作时间为五分钟。
9. · Show the towers to the class, and choose the highest one. · Explain how you make the tower.	9. 各组向全班展示自己的纸塔，选出最高的纸塔，并请该组学生解释为何能够建这么高的纸塔。
10. The instructor's feedback: · Why does no group tear the paper? · Why did some groups use all the paper? · Why can no tower reach the ceiling?	10. 教师向全班同学提问： · 为什么没有人把纸撕掉？ · 为什么有些组把所有的纸都用上了？ · 为什么没有一个塔能够高至天花板？ 然后教师展示如何制作一个可以高达天花板的塔：直接用胶带把纸塔粘到天花板上。

Comments/Reflections

1. This activity can be used for learners at different levels. It can also be used in all kinds of oral classes. The instructor must be skillful in controlling the time and keeping students focusing on the topic since students sometimes are off the given topics.
2. During this activity, students can share their ideas with each other; they can also learn how to state their ideas clearly and logically in public. More importantly, students can learn how to show their agreements and disagreements from working together with their peers.
3. The ceiling-to-floor construction switch provides a dramatic illustration of the importance of reframing. Apparently, this activity can train students to think outside the box. It requires students to discuss the questions from different angles. This will be beneficial for students in their future life and career.

本活动的设计来源于以下文献：Fernandes, James J. (2004). Creative Problem Solving—From Top to Bottom. In Lucas, Stephen E. (ed.) *Selections from the Speech Communication Teacher, 1999–2002*. Madison, Wisconsin: McGraw-Hill. 52–53.

Goal: To use essential real-life problems in speech communication group discussion projects.

Class Size: 25–30 students.

Time: 20–25 mins.

Pre-Class Reading Assignment: Speaking to Persuade (*APS*, Chapter 14, pp. 192–221).

Materials/Preparation: About 10 different topics.

Topics

1. China should abolish English as a compulsory subject at college. Do you agree or disagree with the given statement? State your answer with supporting details.

2. Children of migrant workers should have the same rights to education as local children. Do you agree or disagree with the given statement? State your answer with supporting details.

3. The May Day should not have been shortened. Do you agree or disagree with the given statement? State your answer with supporting details.

4. China should recognize Christmas as an official holiday. Do you agree or disagree with the given statement? State your answer with supporting details.

5. The government should restrict car ownership. Do you agree or disagree with the given statement? State your answer with supporting details.

6. Hugging a stranger can help break down social barriers. Do you agree or disagree with the given statement? State your answer with supporting details.

7. Sex education is appropriate for middle school students. Do you agree or disagree with the given statement? State your answer with supporting details.

8. Housewives should be paid for their work. Do you agree or disagree with the given statement? State your answer with supporting details.

9. A ban on foreign cartoons can boost China's animation industry. Do you agree or disagree with the given statement? State your answer with supporting details.

10. Some famous athletes and entertainers earn millions of dollars every year. Do you think these people deserve such high salaries? Use specific reasons and examples to support your opinion.

PPT/Directions	活动过程描述
1–3 *Directions:* Please read the 10 topics on the PPT carefully, and then each group will send a group member to choose your group topic. Once your group topic has been decided, you cannot change it.	1. 首先教师将全班学生进行分组，每组三至六人。具体情况视班级规模而定。小班三人一组，大班可以是六人一组。 2. 教师要求学生仔细阅读PPT上展示的话题（参见 Materials/Preparation）。 3. 每组派一位代表选择本组的话题。话题选定后不可以更换。
4. Topics	4. 教师向全班同学展示可选的讨论话题，要求全班同学熟悉每一个话题。
5-6 Now every group can begin your group discussion, and try to finish the following tasks: • Define the problem; • Analyze the problem; • Set criteria for a solution; • Explore possible solutions; • Find the best solution; • Make suggestions to improve the solution.	5. 熟悉话题后，小组派代表选择话题，也可以由教师分配话题。分配方法可以是相应的组号对应相应的话题；也可以是逆序，即第一组对应最后一个话题；也可以随机分配。由授课教师自行决定。 6. 请各小组开始小组讨论，需要完成以下内容： • 定义问题； • 分析问题； • 确定解决问题的标准； • 探索解决问题的方法； • 找出解决问题的最佳方法； • 对解决问题的方法加以完善。 讨论时间为八分钟。
7-8 Group Report Time!	7. 小组汇报。邀请一至两组进行汇报，每组汇报时间为五分钟。 8. 教师进行点评。

Comments/Reflections

1. This activity provides students with the opportunity for hands-on investigation on a real-life problem. Some students may not be familiar with the topics in their groups. In this case, the instructor should encourage them to learn about the topics and get to know some ideas from their group members. Learning from the peers is also the purpose of group discussion. In the end, students can benefit a lot by being actively involved in group discussion.

2. This activity is a good way to help students develop critical thinking on hot social issues. It is very effective for students to practice how to speak logically and convincingly. In order to support their

points, students need to adopt some methods. They may use data, examples or theoretic analysis to justify their points of view, which helps improve students' skills in forming a good argument.

本活动的设计基于以下文献：Mandeville, Mary Y. (2001). Using New Approaches in Group Discussion Projects. In Lucas, Stephen E. (ed.) *Selections from the Speech Communication Teacher, 1996–1999*. Madison, Wisconsin: McGraw-Hill. 55–56.

2.3

Who Will Be the Next One to Get off the Boat?

Goal: To make students speak confidently and logically in public.

Class Size: At least 25 students.

Time: 30–35 mins.

Pre-Class Reading Assignment: Organizing the Body of the Speech (*APS*, Chapter 7, pp. 88–101), Outlining the Speech (*APS*, Chapter 9, pp. 118–129).

Materials/Preparation: None.

🕐 In-Class Procedure

PPT/Directions	活动过程描述
1–2 *Directions:* Here's the scenario. Imagine each group on a boat with a hole at its bottom. In order to prevent it from sinking, every five minutes there has to be a member on the boat to jump into the water.	1. 首先将学生分成五组，每个小组最好是五人。 2. 游戏背景：每组学生都被视为各在一艘小船上，小船船底出现了一个小洞。为了不让船沉入江底，每组每隔三分钟将会有一名乘客被选出来跳入江中，以减轻船的重量。现在每位乘客尽量说服其他人自己是最不应该落水的那位，或者说明谁是最应该落水的那位，并给出理由。
3. Everyone will have a chance to persuade others that he or she should stay on the boat. The speaking time for each member is one minute.	3. 每位组员将会有一分钟时间在组内为自己辩护，说明为何自己应该待在船上。 每位组员应该尽量记住同组组员待在船上的理由，或其他人为何应该离开船的理由。
4–5 After four or more rounds, there will be only one person still on the boat. The lucky dog will report to the whole class why he or she was so lucky, while others were chosen to jump into the river.	4. 经过四轮或更多轮回合后（依小组成员而定），每组将会有一位同学幸运地待在船上。 5. 教师请每组的幸运儿代表该组进行小组汇报，讲述本组谁第一位落水，为什么第一位落水的是这个人，为什么自己能够待到最后。 各小组汇报时间为三分钟。
6. Comments.	6. 教师总结整个活动。让学生明白，在公众场合讲话或演讲必须做到有理有据；能够晓之以理，动之以情。

1. This activity is a very good game to train students to speak well without preparation. The speakers will use a lot of presentation skills to win other members' attention or earn their sympathy in order to survive the disaster. Students also need to use a lot of body languages and facial expressions. It's a good way to train students to speak effectively and logically in class.

2. There will be some funny things during this activity. Some students are chosen to get off the boat because the others think they can swim or they are too fat. Some students even suggest that the whole group get off the boat together, and then get on the boat until the rescue comes.

3. Because students don't know who will be the speaker of the group, all of them have to make notes during the group discussion. In addition, the problem arises as to how to present those ideas to the whole class effectively, since some of the reasons are the same. From this activity, students will know that a good speaker is not just to pile up the messages, but to reorganize the messages in a more effective way.

3
UNIT

Note-Taking Training & Listening

UNDERSTANDING TEACHING

The wise ones fashioned speech with their thought, sifting it as grain is sifted through a sieve.

—*Buddha*

All speech, written or spoken, is a dead language, until it finds a willing and prepared hearer.

—*Robert Louis Stevenson*

TEACHER'S GUIDE (Q & A)

➤ **为什么需要记笔记?**

记笔记是为了补充大脑短期记忆和耐久力的不足,以保证听者对演讲内容理解的精准度,并尽可能保证听者获取的演讲信息不受演讲持续时间长短的影响。

一般演讲不会重复多遍。一旦错过、漏过或者突然忘记了某些信息,就不易寻回,因此演讲中的笔记尤为重要。

记笔记还是对演讲者的内容进行再次过滤与思考的过程,可以加深对演讲内容的理解。

➤ **该教学环节何时进行?**

记笔记是作演讲与听演讲非常重要的环节。可以安排在学完演讲的基本理论后,并在准备进行不同类型演讲的学习之前来讲解。笔记既包含演讲前的笔记准备,例如记下演讲的要点或关键词等,类似于演讲的大纲,也包含听别人演讲时如何做笔记,快速记下演讲者的要点,了解演讲的基本结构。

➤ **该教学环节主要学习哪种笔记方法?**

该教学环节主要以口译中的笔记法为主,进行笔记法讲解与学习。口译中的笔记法,一方面能够考查学生的记笔记能力,帮助学生更准确地记下演讲要点与内容;另外一方面,通过进行类似口译训练,让学生把自己记的内容用目标语进行陈述,这是笔记的另一个用途,可以帮助演讲者有效地进行演讲。

➤ 如何记笔记？

- 记笔记的基本原则：
  - 适合自己的笔记方法就是最好的方法，笔记无定法。
  - 笔记所用的语言与符号，可以借鉴别人的，也可以自己发明。
- 笔记的五大要点：
  - 少写多画。少书写汉字，多画线条。
  - 少字多义。一个字可以表达一个甚至几个词的意义。
  - 少线多指。多用自己熟悉的代码来指代要记录的信息。
  - 快速书写。可以是任何字体，只要自己能够看得懂就可以。
  - 明确结束。当记完一段之后，果断结束，以等待记录下一段重要信息。

➤ 如何整理记好的笔记？

- 忆。听完演讲后立即抓紧时间，趁热打铁，对照书本、笔记，及时回忆有关信息。这是整理笔记的重要前提。
- 补。听演讲时所记的笔记，因为是跟着演讲者的速度进行的，而演讲速度要比记录速度快一些，所以笔记会出现缺漏、跳跃、省略等情况，在忆的基础上，及时修补，使笔记更完整。
- 改。仔细审阅你的笔记，对错字、错句及其他不够确切的地方进行修改。
- 编。用统一的序号，对笔记内容进行提纲式的、逻辑性的排列，注明号码，梳理好笔记的先后顺序。
- 分。以文字（最好用彩色笔）或符号、代号等划分笔记内容的类别。例如：哪些是字词类，哪些是作家与作品类，哪些是作品（或课文）分析类，哪些是问题质疑、探索类等。
- 舍。省略无关紧要的笔记内容，使笔记简明扼要。
- 记。分类抄录经过整理的笔记。同类的知识，摘抄在同一个本子上或一个本子的同一部分，也可以用卡片分类抄录，以方便日后查阅，按需所取，纲目清晰，快捷好用，便于记忆。

➤ 常见的教学困难

- 学生不重视记笔记，上课不记笔记，以为课后可以拷贝教师的讲义；听别人演讲时，不记笔记，认为可以用手机录音甚至录像。
- 学生很难找到合适的训练材料。
- 学生缺乏自己创造代码与符号的创造力。

➤ 教与学的误区

- 认为演讲中，笔记没有作用，尤其是对普通听众而言。实际上，在演讲中，听众记笔记非常有必要。首先，一般演讲结束后，会有提问环节，如果有些信息不清楚，提问题就不能切中要害。其次，采用电子设备录音或者录像，会受到现场及周边环境等外界因素的干扰，有时还会出现人为操作失误。
- 认为记笔记是没办法训练的。记笔记是一门熟能生巧的技能，多记笔记，记笔记的速度自然会加快，准确度也会提高。

ACTIVITIES

3.1

Learn to Use Your Own Symbols or Abbreviations to Take Notes

Goal: To train students to form a habit of taking notes by applying the symbols or abbreviations that they are familiar with.

Class Size: 25–30 students.

Time: 25–30 mins.

Pre-Class Reading Assignment: Speaking to Inform (*APS*, Chapter 13, pp. 176–191).

Materials/Preparation: Sample notes and the speech script on which the notes are based*.

Script and Sample Notes 1

Script:

It is estimated that in 2003, China will become the third largest online market in the Asia-Pacific region with sales of over 56 million US dollars. It is expected that in the next few years, the software and information service industries in China will maintain their growth rate of over 30%. To achieve this target, we face serious challenges. First, we must break through the bottleneck of bandwidth.

Notes:

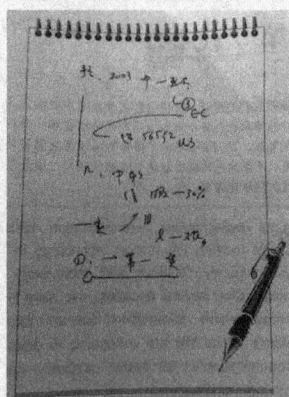

Script and Sample Notes 2

Script:

We must accelerate the development of our R&D as well as our production capabilities with super capacity, advanced technology, flexibility as well as efficiency, and an economy of scale. We must achieve breakthroughs in application as well as integration, coordination and interactive sharing. Our priority has to be the transformation of traditional industries, driving forward information on all fronts. The information industry in China forms the basis for information. It is also part of the process.

Notes:

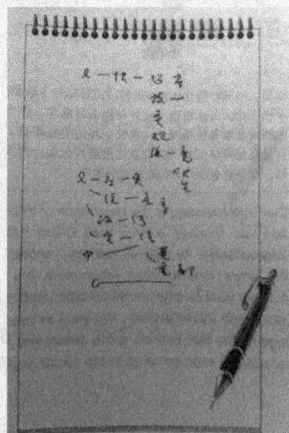

* 引自林超伦（英）.（2004）.《实践口译》.北京：外语教学与研究出版社. PP. 166–170.

PPT/Directions	活动过程描述
1–2 Form Groups	1. 全班学生分成八个小组，每组三至四位成员。 2. 每两组间将进行比赛。比赛顺序为： 第1组 vs. 第2组 第3组 vs. 第4组 第5组 vs. 第6组 第7组 vs. 第8组
3–5 Note-Taking Competition	3. 参赛的两组同时听一篇演讲，由教师朗读，只读一遍。参赛组员记笔记。 4. 每组推选一位代表在黑板上展示自己的笔记，并且尽可能详细地解释笔记内容。 5. 各组展示结束后，教师向全班展示原始的笔记。
6. Speech for the First Round	6. 第一轮比赛。 教师可以自己朗读或请一位学生朗读Materials/Preparation中Script and Sample Notes 1的脚本。
7. Discussion	7. 演讲结束后，小组开始讨论，并决定推选展示笔记的代表。
8–9 Notes Explanation	8. 讨论结束后，请第一组的代表上场，第二组的代表在教室外候场。 9. 第一组代表展示并解释结束后，邀请第二组的代表出场展示并解释内容。
10. 	10. 教师展示样板笔记。

（待续）

PPT/Directions	活动过程描述
11. Who is the winner and who is the loser?	11. 决定谁是胜方。
12. The Second Round	12. 第二轮活动规则同第一轮活动一样。
13. Basic Note-Taking Skills	13. 最后，教师介绍基本的记笔记技巧给学生。

Comments/Reflections

1. This activity is especially recommended when the students are translation and interpreting majors. Otherwise, one or two such intensive training would be fine. More typically, notes of an outline or very important details may suffice. Instructors should also make sure that the audience and the speaker have enough eye contact.

2. During this activity, students often forget the meaning of the symbols or abbreviations they created during the speech. The instructor should remind students in advance to choose symbols or abbreviations they can easily recognize or identify.

3. This activity helps students understand the importance of taking notes and the importance of the organization of a speech. This is helpful for them to appreciate speeches or give speeches themselves.

Peer Evaluation

UNDERSTANDING TEACHING

In learning you will teach, and in teaching you will learn.

—Phil Collins

You cannot teach a man anything, you can only help him find it within himself.

—Galileo Galilei

To know how to suggest is the art of teaching.

—Henri-Frédéric Amiel

TEACHER'S GUIDE (Q & A)

➤ **同伴互评的定义是什么?**

- 同伴互评（peer evaluation/feedback，也称同伴反馈）是一种合作学习机制，是与教师反馈（teacher's feedback）相对而言的。
- 同伴互评指的是由学生对彼此完成学习任务的情况进行互评，是一种建立在建构主义理论和外语习得理论基础上的学习活动。在大学英语演讲教学过程中，同伴互评可以改变学生学习英语演讲过程中被动学习的现状，通过同伴间的交互和共同构建，消除学生对英语演讲的焦虑和恐惧，提高学生英语社交和认知的技能，增强学生对英语演讲的兴趣，有助于教师实施针对性的指导，从而进一步激发学生学习英语演讲的主动性和创造性。

➤ **影响同伴互评的因素有哪些?**

- 文化因素
  中国学生最突出的特点是不爱说话，经常保留对其他群组成员构成伤害的评价。他们总是在不伤害他人情感和直接表达自己的看法之间寻找平衡。为了不使对方难堪，他们会隐瞒自己的真实意见。当和同伴意见相左时，因为担心会冒犯或惹怒同伴，他们也会保留自己的意见。另外，学生觉得自己不具备教师的权威，缺乏作为同伴演讲评论者所需的专业知识，因而不愿意提出批评意见。

- 主观能动因素

  有些学生对同伴互评认识不够，缺乏责任心。他们只是把同伴互评当作教师布置的一项任务，在讨论中缺乏互评的积极性，互评时难以给出具体细致的评论，只提出总体评论如"Good!"或"Well done!"，使评论流于表面形式。

- 评价主体的技能因素

  英语基础较弱的学生很难发现同伴演讲中的问题，有些学生在评价中仅能发现一些表层错误，如语法错误、发音错误，很少有学生能评论演讲的主题陈述、结构安排、连贯性及语言的清晰度、风格、逻辑等问题，在如何使演讲更有层次和更有内涵方面更是束手无策。另外，当学生对某些问题不确定，无法判断正确与否，或在讨论中意见不一致时，他们很难给出恰如其分的评论。

➤ 该章节何时进行？

本章节没有一个固定的讲解时间，一般都随堂进行，也可以在每次课堂演讲时都开展这样的活动。但第一次进行该活动应该在学生学完《演讲的艺术》第十版（中国版）第一至三章后，让学生对英语演讲有基本的理论认识的前提下进行。如果是对学生的介绍性演讲进行同伴互评，那可以在安排学生进行介绍性演讲时，让学生随堂进行。但是进行该活动前，教师要先向学生简要介绍评估计划，讲解评估标准。

➤ 常见的教学困难

- 学生对于同伴互评的认可和接受程度会直接影响同伴互评的实践。有研究表明学生不赞成同伴互评，认为这有利于英语演讲水平较低的学生，而不利于水平较高的学生。且学生通常不愿给自己的同学太高或太低的分数。

- 学生抱怨这种活动毫无用处，认为自己没有评价的能力，自己的语言水平不足以完成互评活动。

➤ 教与学的误区

- 大多数学生认为这是给自己同学挑刺或找错的事情。实际上，同伴互评也可以是表扬的评价。对大多数学生而言，同伴互评是一种学习的过程，取人之所长补己之所短。

- 担心同学评价不权威、不专业。对同学的演讲进行评价也是一种学习过程，有则改之，无则加勉。

Peer Evaluation on Introductory Speech

4.1

Goal: To develop students' ability of evaluating speeches, help students internalize public speaking principles and strategies, and eventually improve their public speaking skills.

Class Size: 26–30 students.

Time: 50 mins.

Pre-Class Reading Assignment: Delivering the Speech (*APS*, Chapter 11, pp. 146–158); Speaking on Special Occasions (*APS*, Chapter 15, pp. 222–232).

Materials/Preparation: A. Introductory Speech Evaluation Form. The number of evaluation forms will be two times that of the students. For example, if there are 26 students, the instructor needs to prepare 52 copies.

Introductory Speech Evaluation Form

Speaker: _____

Topic: _____

Rate the speaker on each point:

5–Excellent 4–Good 3–Average 2–Fair 1–Poor

1. Introduction gained attention	5 4 3 2 1
2. Subject introduced clearly	5 4 3 2 1
3. Main ideas easily followed	5 4 3 2 1
4. Language clear	5 4 3 2 1
5. Language vivid	5 4 3 2 1
6. Topic dealt with creatively	5 4 3 2 1
7. Strong conclusion	5 4 3 2 1
8. Speech adapted to audience	5 4 3 2 1
9. Sufficient eye contact	5 4 3 2 1
10. Voice used effectively	5 4 3 2 1
11. Non verbal communication effective	5 4 3 2 1
12. Overall evaluation of the speech	5 4 3 2 1

Comments: (Either in Chinese or English)

_____

_____

B. Video of Klaus Schwab's introductory speech about Bill Gates (available on heep. unipus. cn).

C. Students need to prepare a two-minute introductory speech in advance.

🕐 In-Class Procedure

PPT/Directions	活动过程描述
1–2 Get to know the criteria for evaluating introductory speeches.	1. 教师向全体学生介绍评估标准（参见 Materials/Preparation A），时间为5–8分钟。 2. 教师向全班同学发评估表，每位学生两份。（一份用来评估教师在课堂上播放的视频；一份用来对同学进行评估。）
3–5 Appreciate and evaluate a video of introductory speech.	3. 教师给学生播放施瓦布先生关于比尔·盖茨的介绍性演讲（参见 Materials/Preparation B）。 4. 带领学生利用评估标准针对施瓦布先生的演讲进行示范评估。 5. 给学生五分钟时间完成评估训练。
6–7 Show the class your evaluation of the speech.	6. 教师选择一至两位同学向全班展示自己的评估。每位同学展示时间为2–3分钟。 7. 教师就学生的评估进行简要评价。
8. After being familiar with the criteria for evaluating introductory speeches, students will be divided into pairs.	8. 教师在学生了解完评估标准后，快速将全班学生分为两人一组。
9. The first round practice of peer evaluation: 1) A student gives his or her introductory speech in front of his or her partner. 2) The listener will do the evaluation job by writing on another evaluation form in details after the speech. 3) The listener will give the oral feedback to the speaker. And give the evaluation form to the speaker.	9. 第一回合同伴互评： 1）每组中一位学生向搭档进行两分钟的介绍性演讲。 2）作为听众的学生，在听演讲的过程中进行相关记录，并在演讲结束后完成另外一张演讲评估表。 3）评估结束后，听众一方根据自己完成的演讲评估表，向搭档（演讲者）进行口头反馈，最后将评估表交给演讲者。（口头反馈时间不能超过五分钟。）

（待续）

PPT/Directions	活动过程描述
10. The second round of peer evaluation: The roles will be changed. The speaker in the first round will be the listener in the second round, while the listener will be the speaker. The process of the activity will be the same as the first round.	10. 第二回合，每组学生角色互换，即第一回合的演讲者此回合为听众，第一回合的听众此回合则为演讲者。活动步骤与过程同第一回合。
11. After these two rounds, students are to modify their introductory speech after class according to their partners' written and oral feedback. And prepare the presentation of the speech next class.	11. 在两个回合活动结束后，教师要求学生按照收到的书面及口头反馈，对自己的演讲进行修改完善，以准备下一次的课堂演讲。

Comments/Reflections

1. To activate peer evaluation, students should be divided into different pairs, and the pairs should remain largely fixed so that the partners could get to know each other and feel free to exchange ideas. A better understanding of each other and each other's speech would ensure the consistency of the in-group peer evaluation. So in the real practice of my class, students will form into pairs at the beginning of the term. This will help them feel free to give feedback and discuss the problems in the speech.

2. Obviously, there will be some drawbacks of this activity. The first one is it will be so noisy when all pairs begin to speak in the classroom at the same time. It is not helpful for the listener to exactly understand the speaker. It is not comfortable for the speaker to fully perform during the speech as well. So the instructor can allow students to stand more closely to their partners. Another drawback will be the partners' English level. It is no doubt that students' English levels will be different. Some will have a partner who has very good language proficiency, while others will not. So the instructor will have a macro management of the match of pairs, and change the member of each pair every month during the whole semester for peer evaluation.

（供稿人：时丽娜 复旦大学；改编人：周红兵）

4.2 Peer Evaluation on the Class Recitation

Goal: To help students learn how to evaluate a speech, how to appreciate classic speeches and how to make full use of their verbal and nonverbal communication skills.

Class Size: 25–30 students.

Time: 45 mins.

Reading Assignment: Using Language & Delivering the Speech (*APS*, Chapter 10 & 11, pp. 130–158).

Materials/Preparation:
A. Recitation Evaluation Form. The number of evaluation forms will be three times that of the students. If there are 25 students, the instructor needs to prepare 75 copies.

Recitation Evaluation Form

Speaker: _____

Topic: _____

Rate the speaker on each point:

5–Excellent 4–Good 3–Average 2–Fair 1–Poor

1. Volume	5	4	3	2	1
2. Pitch	5	4	3	2	1
3. Rate	5	4	3	2	1
4. Pause	5	4	3	2	1
5. Vocal variety	5	4	3	2	1
6. Pronunciation	5	4	3	2	1
7. Articulation	5	4	3	2	1
8. Personal appearance	5	4	3	2	1
9. Movement/gestures	5	4	3	2	1
10. Eye contact	5	4	3	2	1
11. Overall evaluation of the speech	5	4	3	2	1

Comments: (Either in Chinese or English)

_____

_____

B. Students need to prepare to recite a two-minute excerpt from their favorite classic speech in advance, and bring the audio or video of the classic speech to the class.

PPT/Directions	活动过程描述
1. Get to know the criteria for evaluating recitations.	1. 教师向全体学生介绍评估标准（参见 Materials/Preparation A），时间为5–8分钟。
2–4 The class will be divided into several groups and each will contain four members. Everyone will have three Recitation Evaluation Forms.	2. 教师将全班分为若干小组，每组人数最好是四人。 3. 教师向全班同学发评估表，每位学生三份。 4. 教师讲解三份评估表的作用，用来在小组内给每位组员的模拟背诵进行评估。
5. Recitation in each group: 1) Every member of the group will recite the excerpt from their favorite classic speech in turn. 2) The recitation will be two minutes. 3) Every member of the group will give the speaker's recitation a detailed evaluation within three minutes.	5. 小组内的经典片段背诵： 　1）每位组员背诵自己节选的经典演讲。 　2）每位组员对小组内除本人外的所有背诵者进行书面评估。 　3）每位组员背诵完后，全组将会有三分钟时间完成书面评估。然后进行下一个背诵。整个小组的活动时间为15–20分钟。
6–8 · Collect feedback. · Prepare for class presentation.	6. 各个组员从其他组员那里获得自己的背诵评估。 7. 各个组员根据同学的评估，进行调整练习，准备进行班级背诵表演。这部分时间为五分钟。 8. 全组选出一位代表在全班进行背诵表演。
9. Choose the best recitation.	9. 班内背诵活动： 　1）每组代表轮流上台进行背诵（每人两分钟）。 　2）所有代表背诵结束后，各小组进行简要讨论，选出最佳背诵表演者。
10. Comments and suggestions from the instructor.	10. 教师最后对整堂课进行总结，并提出改进建议。

1. A flexible and diversified peer evaluation model can be established. Each round of peer evaluation adopts a unique format. It boosts students' interpersonal communication skills and provides them with more opportunities to evaluate speeches of various styles by multiple peers.

2. Integrated with teacher's evaluation and self-evaluation, peer evaluation can be oral or written or both, and it can be done in English or Chinese. To ensure its reliability and validity, and to maximize its diagnostic and stimulative values, peer evaluation should be persuasive with specific cases. Completed evaluation forms are handed back to students to help them with their self-evaluation.

3. Peer evaluation is a demanding task for the instructor who should play the multiple roles of a supervisor, an organizer, a guide, a leader, a facilitator and a coordinator during the whole process. But it is also a rewarding task for both students and the instructor.

(供稿人：时丽娜 复旦大学；改编人：周红兵)

Teacher's Feedback

UNDERSTANDING TEACHING

The mediocre teacher tells. The good teacher explains. The superior teacher demonstrates. The great teacher inspires.

—William Arthur Ward

Those who know, do. Those that understand, teach.

—Aristotle

TEACHER'S GUIDE (Q & A)

➤ **教师反馈的定义是什么?**

      教师反馈主要是指课堂中教师接受、拒绝、评估学生的反应,可以通过赞同、表扬、否定、纠错、沉默等形式来表现。教师反馈是课堂交际结构中不可或缺的组成部分,是优化教学过程,实现教与学和谐统一的必不可少的环节。如在学生回答问题后,教师说的"对,很好"等评语;教师对学生的语法错误皱眉头;学生的考试成绩;教师给学生作业的批改评语等,均是教师反馈在实践中的不同表现。

➤ **教师反馈的形式有哪些?**

- 教师反馈可以是书面的或口头的;
- 教师反馈可以是有声的或无声的;
- 教师反馈可以是对正确的肯定,也可以是对错误的指正。

➤ **教师反馈的种类有哪些?**

- 评估性与话语性反馈
  - 评估性反馈主要是评估功能,仅对学生应答所提供信息的正确性进行评判。
  - 话语性反馈的侧重点在语言内容而非形式上,常与参考型问题并用。
- 积极反馈与消极反馈
  - 积极反馈是指教师对学生输出的确认,即用肯定的话语对学生的应答表示赞同、肯定,如"Good"、"Yes"、"OK"、"Wonderful"、"Excellent"和"Well done"

等。它可以进一步分为简单积极反馈（比如重复学生回答或者说"Good"）、积极反馈加点评和积极反馈加启发，以引起学生更多的输出。

- 消极反馈是指当学习者的回答有不合规范或者不当之处时，教师对学习者输出的否认。狭义来讲，就是指教师对学生所犯错误的反应，即纠正性反馈。其分类如下：

  显性纠错：直接纠错；元语言反馈，即利用语言知识进行反思。

  隐性纠错：重复——以升调对错误的语言形式加以重复；澄清请求——要求学习者改正错误形式；重铸——通过变换一个或多个句子成分（主语、谓语或宾语）重释话语，原意保留不变；提示——重复学生部分话语，以试图引出正确形式。

➤ 常见的教学困难

- 一些教师本身缺乏教师反馈技巧，在对学生进行反馈或纠错时，缺乏技巧与艺术性，从而让学生产生一定的反感与不配合；还有的教师反馈，从第一堂开始到最后一堂课都是一样的。

- 现在的大学里面，因为很多都是大班教学，教师在反馈尤其是书面反馈时，工作量特别大。建议教师每次对班内一个小组进行详细反馈，其他小组实行简单反馈，这样一个学期可以对全班每位学生进行一次详细反馈。

➤ 教与学的误区

- 教师认为反馈就是纠错，就是给学生打分。课堂反馈的形式不只这些，课堂反馈是一门艺术，适当的、得体的课堂反馈将对促进课堂教学起到巨大的作用。

- 经常进行全班集体反馈。实际上，教师在课堂反馈的时候应该做到点面结合，既有全班的共性问题的提出，也有对个体学生的点评。

Teacher's Feedback on Informative Speech

5.1

Goal:	To help students understand the principles of informative speech.
Class Size:	20–25 students.
Time:	90 mins.
Reading Assignment:	Delivering the Speech (*APS*, Chapter 11, pp.146–158); Speaking to Inform (*APS*, Chapter 13, pp. 176–191).
Materials/Preparation:	A. Informative Speech Evaluation Form and a video camera. A pre-class check is needed to make sure that the camera works properly.

Informative Speech Evaluation Form

Speaker: _____

Topic: _____

Rate the speaker on each point:

5–Excellent   4–Good   3–Average   2–Fair   1–Poor

1.	Topic well-chosen and interesting	5	4	3	2	1
2.	Introduction clear and attractive	5	4	3	2	1
3.	Main points clear	5	4	3	2	1
4.	Main points fully supported	5	4	3	2	1
5.	Organization well planned	5	4	3	2	1
6.	Conclusion natural and vivid	5	4	3	2	1
7.	Central idea reinforced	5	4	3	2	1
8.	Eye contact	5	4	3	2	1
9.	Vocal variety	5	4	3	2	1
10.	Pace and pause	5	4	3	2	1
11.	Visual aids well-presented	5	4	3	2	1
12.	Speech adapted to audience	5	4	3	2	1
13.	Overall evaluation of the speech	5	4	3	2	1

Comments:

_____

_____

_____

B. Video clip: "Yoga: United Mind, Body and Spirit" (*APS*, Video 13.3).

C. Students need to prepare a three-minute informative speech a week in advance.

In-Class Procedure

PPT/Directions	活动过程描述
1. Get to know the criteria for evaluating informative speeches and how to evaluate an informative speech.	1. 教师向全班学生介绍评估标准（参见 Materials/Preparation A），时间约为五分钟。
2–4 Video of informative speech—"Yoga: United Mind, Body, and Spirit."	2. 教师给学生播放视频"Yoga: United Mind, Body and Spirit"（参见 Materials/Preparation B）。 3. 教师参照评估表对视频中的示范演讲进行逐条评估（此时教师应该把评估表通过投影向全班展示）。 4. 教师的整个示范评估时间不能超过五分钟。
5–6 The informative speech presentation: Students come to the stage to make a three-minute informative speech.	5. 课堂演讲开始，教师在学生开始演讲前，要准备好纸质的评估表，教师需要对每位学生进行评估。 6. 在学生正式演讲前，打开摄像机。
7. The first speaker begins his or her speech.	7. 学生演讲开始，教师邀请第一位演讲者上台。每位学生演讲时间是三分钟，教师记得提醒学生演讲的时间。
8–9 Individual feedback.	8. 每位演讲者的演讲结束后，教师都要完成自己对该演讲者的评价。 9. 同时，教师要对演讲进行录像。
10. Overall feedback.	10. 在所有学生完成演讲之后，教师进行整体口头点评，针对具体情况，根据评估标准依次进行逐项反馈，同时列举几个典型例子加以说明。

（待续）

PPT/Directions	活动过程描述
11. Written feedback together with the speech video.	11. 书面反馈： 教师填写评估表（教师反馈应尽量详细周全），如果有不确定的地方，教师可以再次观看录像，进行确认，并在下一次课时和演讲录像等一起返还学生。让学生进行自我评估，也可对教师的评估提出质疑。

Comments/Reflections

1. Record students' speeches only. Make separate files for each speaker for after-class reflection.

2. Closely related to students' peer evaluation and self-evaluation, the teacher's feedback is often given in two forms, oral and written. Oral feedback is given on the overall performance or on the individual speeches.

3. The combination of oral feedback and written feedback reinforces students' understanding of their own strengths and weaknesses, promotes students' mastery of effective public speaking principles, and eventually boosts their speaking skills. Meanwhile, the feedback mechanism helps insturctors make timely and constant adaptation to the course and thus improve their expertise.

(供稿人：时丽娜 复旦大学；改编人：周红兵)

5.2   Teacher's Feedback on Persuasive Speech

Goal: To help students understand the differences between persuasive speech and other speeches, and be skillful in persuading the public.

Class Size: 20–25 students.

Time: 45 mins.

Reading Assignment: Delivering the Speech (*APS*, Chapter 11, pp.146–158); Speaking to Persuade (*APS*, Chapter 14, pp. 192–221).

Materials/Preparation: A.   Persuasive Speech Evaluation Form.

Persuasive Speech Evaluation Form

Speaker: _____

Topic: _____

Specific Purpose: _____

Rate the speaker on each point:

5–Excellent   4–Good   3–Average   2–Fair   1–Poor

Introduction

1. Gained attention and interest	5 4 3 2 1
2. Introduced topic clearly	5 4 3 2 1
3. Established credibility	5 4 3 2 1
4. Previewed body of speech	5 4 3 2 1
5. Related topic to audience	5 4 3 2 1

Body

6. Main points clear	5 4 3 2 1
7. Organization well planned	5 4 3 2 1
8. Sufficient evidence	5 4 3 2 1
9. Evidence from qualified sources	5 4 3 2 1
10. Reasoning clear and sound	5 4 3 2 1
11. Language clear and concise	5 4 3 2 1
12. Connectives effective	5 4 3 2 1

Conclusion

13. Prepared audience for ending	5 4 3 2 1
14. Reinforced central idea	5 4 3 2 1
15. Vivid ending	5 4 3 2 1

Delivery

16. Began speech without rushing	5 4 3 2 1

17. Maintained strong eye contact	5	4	3	2 1
18. Avoided distracting mannerisms	5	4	3	2 1
19. Articulated words clearly	5	4	3	2 1
20. Used pauses effectively	5	4	3	2 1
21. Used vocal variety to add impact	5	4	3	2 1
22. Presented visual aids well (optional)	5	4	3	2 1
23. Communicated enthusiasm for topic	5	4	3	2 1

Comments:

_____

_____

_____

B. Video clip: "Making a Difference Through the Special Olympics" (*APS*, Video 14.4).

C. Students need to prepare a five-minute persuasive speech in advance. The instructor should assign the speech task to students two weeks earlier than the speech day.

In-Class Procedure

PPT/Directions	活动过程描述
1. Criteria for evaluating persuasive speeches.	1. 教师向全班学生介绍评估标准（参见 Materials/ Preparation A），时间约为五分钟。
2–4 Video of persuasive speech—"Making a Difference Through the Special Olympics."	2. 教师给学生播放视频 "Making a Difference Through the Special Olympics"（参见 Materials/ Preparation B）。 3. 教师参照评估表对视频中的示范演讲进行逐条评估（此时教师应该把评估表通过投影向全班展示）。 4. 教师的整个示范评估时间不能超过五分钟。
5–8 • First speech (up to five mins.). • Comments.	5. 教师邀请第一位演讲者上台演讲，时间为五分钟。 6. 演讲者在演讲时，教师需要根据演讲者实际表现，对其进行评估。 7. 演讲者演讲结束后，教师向全班点评该演讲。 8. 教师的点评时间应该控制在五分钟以内。

（待续）

PPT/Directions	活动过程描述
9. • Second speech. • Comments.	9. 然后第二位演讲者上台。教师的评估过程同上。
10. • Last speech. • Overall feedback.	10. 所有学生演讲结束后，教师将对整堂课进行总结，并提出意见与建议。

Comments/Reflections

1. Oral feedback is mainly analytic and diagnostic commentary. Before each type of speech is given, the instructor should inform students of the major requirements and criteria, lead them through one or two sample speeches by exemplifying how to give proper oral feedback.

2. When the instructor is doing the oral feedback in class, the tone should be mild, not too sharp. The comment should be made with concrete examples, so it is apparent that this is a big challenge for every instructor.

3. Written feedback is mainly targeted at individual speeches as complementary to the oral feedback which has a more direct impact on students. Instructors are suggested to fill out the evaluation form designed for each type of speech for each student and then return it to him or her. Written feedback is beneficial to instructors. Kept on file, it can serve as a significant reference for course development as well as first-hand material for academic research. Written feedback is also significant to students who have awkward body language, embarrassing verbal expressions or severe pronunciation defects, etc., which would be impossible to point out orally in class without hurting students' feelings or self-confidence. In these cases, written feedback would be a much better solution.

(供稿人：时丽娜 复旦大学；改编人：周红兵)

Large Class

UNDERSTANDING TEACHING

Learning is finding out what you already know. Doing is demonstrating that you know it. Teaching is reminding others that they know just as well as you. You are all learners, doers, instructors.

—*Richard Bach*

Kids don't remember what you try to teach them. They remember what you are.

—*Jim Henson*

TEACHER'S GUIDE (Q & A)

➤ **多少学生的班级算大班?**

- 美国高校的公众演讲课堂,较为典型的班级为十几人的小班。从中国高校的演讲教学实践来看,一般25人以下的班可视为较为典型的小班。大班人数一般在40人以上,部分高校可能在60–100人之间,个别的可能出现200人左右的超大班。

- 虽均称之为大班,但40–60人的课堂与100–200人的课堂的授课方式必然有所不同。同时,虽授课及课堂组织方式不同,但教学目的、课堂组织原则等方面却是一样的。

➤ **大班教学中的主要困难表现在哪些地方?**

- 如何选择授课方式?是以讲座为主还是以班级或小组的演讲实践活动为主?如何能让所有人都感兴趣?

- 如何组织课堂活动?表现为两方面:
  第一,从时间把握上,如何为每一位学生提供参与小组活动的机会?
  第二,在演讲者只能是极少数,而绝大部分学生为听众的情况下,如何防止听众对台上的演讲失去兴趣,转而做自己的事情,甚至出现逃课现象?学生若无参与感,则很容易失去学习兴趣。

- 是否需要保证为每名学生提供演讲实践的机会?如何实现?

- 大班的考核如何进行?如何进行评估?

➤ 大班教学的优势在哪里?

- 大班与小班相比，人气旺是最明显的优势。"公众"演讲常需要"公众"的配合，一旦听众学生的积极性受到激发，上课效果甚至比小班更好。
- 大班一定能够挖掘出几位演讲天才或热衷于演讲的学生，他们对全班的影响力不可低估。如果让这些学生发挥作用，会有力地活跃课堂气氛。

➤ 大班教学的误区

- 演讲课的最终目的在于演讲实践，大班无法提供给每一位学生演讲机会，因此，大班无法进行演讲教学。
- 大班只合适进行讲座，"讲授"公众演讲知识或欣赏经典演讲（片段），不能组织演讲实践。
- 如果不在课堂上进行演讲实践，学生就没有演讲实践的感受；而没有演讲实践的感受，就等于没有上演讲课。

➤ 大班教学的几点建议

- 本活动手册中绝大部分课堂活动（班级规模"Class Size"无限制，标为"Any"的活动）都适用于40人左右的班级。活动细节稍为调整，也大多适用于60人左右的班级。
- 大班教学可以考虑以讲座为主（但并不排除以小组活动的实践方式为主）。例如，可以采取学期前三分之二的时间以演讲案例分析的形式，讲解公众演讲的理论知识，后三分之一的时间组织演讲实践。
- 建议教师在第一次课上向学生布置学期演讲任务，包括演讲稿写作和演讲表达，并在每次理论讲解之后，让学生完成相应的步骤。
- 需充分发挥优秀学生的带头作用，组织小组活动，包括课堂活动与课后作业。
- 充分利用同伴互评的方式，一方面增加学生的参与感，一方面让学生在评估中学习和进步。
- 网络教学建议：
  A. 目前的网络教学发展为大班的演讲课提供了有力的技术支持，使得大班演讲教学的效果得到保证。其中最有力的技术支持包括学生演讲视频上传，以及学生的互评平台系统。
  B. 在技术支持下，大班的演讲课也可以像小班那样。理论讲解（建议采用微型讲座，mini-lecture）之后，可布置演讲实践任务。课后，学生将自己的演讲录制成视频，然后上传至网络平台。鼓励多次录制，直到满意为止。每位学生有义务观看并点评随机分配的数段演讲。教师从学生评估结果中抽取典型演讲样例，并在下一次课上作为分析材料。
  C. 演讲考核也可采用类似方法。教师评估与学生互评相结合。
  D. 网络技术在不断发展，教师也可根据自己的需求，请技术部门协助实现。同时，技术的发展也离不开教师的需求和想象。有些教师问："技术能为我们做什么？"技术人员会回答："你们想让我们做什么？"
  E. 这里推荐外研社制作的《演讲的艺术》数字课程。课程不仅包括基础知识，还包括赏析、作业和分享平台等。

What's Wrong with the Speech? Understanding the Contents of the Course Based on a Case Study.

6.1

Goal: To exhibit a big picture of what students are expected to learn in this course at the beginning of the semester by allowing them an opportunity to see the differences between a need-improvement speech and the final version of the speech.

Class Size: 60 students.

Time: 6 mins. + 40 mins.

Pre-Class Reading Assignment: A. Contents (*APS*, xvi–xxv).

B. "Securing Yourself Online" (Need-Improvement Version). Read the script carefully and watch the video (*APS Teacher's Manual*, pp. 250–251; also *Speeches for Analysis and Discussion DVD*).

Materials/Preparation: A. A sample need-improvement version of an American student's speech (taken from *APS Teacher's Manual*, pp. 250–251; also *Speeches for Analysis and Discussion DVD*).

Securing Yourself Online (Need-Improvement Version)

1 Okay, ready? How much do you know about computer security problems? They're really serious, especially for college students like us. You wouldn't believe how many computers are infected and compromised.

2 I've always been interested in computers, and I use mine all the time. So today I'm going to talk about computer safety and explain some things you can do to secure yourself when you're online.

3 First, you should use a strong password. What makes a strong password? Take a look at this example. Okay, that's it. Here's the right one. This is a long password, which is good. You need lots of characters. All my sources say that this will help keep you safe.

4 Using a secure connection is important, too. That means your connection is encrypted. How do you know if your connection is secure? Here are two screen shots I copied from my computer. This one shows a secure connection. It says *https* at the top. You may not be able to see it, but it will keep you safe.

5 Here's an insecure connection. As you can see, it doesn't have an *s*— there, after the *http*.

6   It also helps to double-check links before you click them. Sometimes you get e-mails like this one from your bank or someone pretending to be your bank. But the e-mail is not really from your bank; it's from a hacker who wants your financial information. If you check this out before clicking on the link, you can save yourself a lot of trouble and also maybe a lot of money.

7   So, I guess that's it. Protecting yourself online is extremely important in today's world. I hope you know more about this as a result of my speech.

B. A detailed analysis of the need-improvement speech (adapted from *APS Teacher's Manual*, pp. 251–252).

Parts	Analysis: Aspects Where Improvement Is Needed
Introduction Paras. 1 & 2	Not effective/interesting enough.
Para. 1	1) He has no eye contact when approaching the lectern. 2) He keeps his head down, pulling his notes out of his back pocket, and starting talking before making sure the audience is paying attention. 3) The opening words, "Okay, ready," do not provide an effective attention-getter. 4) He reveals the topic and tries to relate the topic to his audience by noting that computer security problems are "really serious," especially for college students. (Good; but not as effective as the final version which is supported by strong evidence.)
Para. 2	1) He does not well establish his credibility on the topic of online security by his being interested in computers and using it all the time. Expert knowledge is required. 2) The preview is well done; but it would be better if concrete information about the points were given.
Body Paras. 3–6	1) Main points are underdeveloped. 2) Visual aids are poorly designed. 3) The delivery is not strong enough to boost his credibility or to get the audience engaged in the speech.
Para. 3	1) When he discusses the importance of having a strong password, the PowerPoint slide is almost impossible to read. 2) He displays a textbook example of how not to use PowerPoint: the composition of the slide, the color scheme, the choice of font, the unnecessary use of clip art, and the speaker's confusion about which slide he is displaying. 3) The problem is compounded by the speaker's failure to provide an adequate explanation of the slide. He states that a strong password should contain "lots of characters," but he does not indicate how many characters that might be. Nor does he cite any sources that support the importance of a strong password.

（待续）

Parts	Analysis: Aspects Where Improvement Is Needed
Paras. 4 & 5	This main point focuses on the need for students to use a secure connection when they are online. Again, the speaker uses PowerPoint so badly when illustrating his point with it. 1) The slides are too small and too cluttered to communicate his point. 2) Moreover, as in Main Point 1, he fails to provide a satisfactory explanation of his slide.
Para. 6	This main point stresses the importance of double-checking links before clicking on them. 1) This is important information, but the speaker does not explain it clearly. 2) His PowerPoint slide is too small to be seen clearly. 3) In contrast, the final version of the speech uses two large, well-designed slides in this section, and the speaker goes through his points step by step to make sure the audience understands them.
Conclusion Para. 7	The speech concludes in Para. 7 and reinforces the perception that the speaker is not fully prepared.
Para. 7	1) He does not prepare the audience for the ending. 2) Not only is the content weak, but the delivery is halting and tentative. 3) Because the speaker forgot to exit from the PowerPoint slide he displayed in Main Point 3, that slide is still on display during his conclusion. He discovers his error as he is leaving the lectern, and he dashes back to turn off the slide, but because he did not insert a blank slide at the end of his presentation, he cannot clear the screen before returning to his seat.
Others	1) The speaker wears very casual attire, which leaves an impression that he's not very serious about the job. (Physical appearance.) 2) Language is less formal or accurate compared with the final version. 3) Poor communicative skills results from failure in audience analysis, for example, how to make the information clear enough for the audience to understand. 4) Transitions and connectives are not effective enough. (Need to compare with the final version.)

C. A sample final version of the speech (taken from *APS Teacher's Manual*, pp. 253–254; also *Speeches for Analysis and Discussion DVD*).

Securing Yourself Online (Final Version)

1 You are at risk. All of us are at risk. I'm not talking about STDs, global warming, or terrorism. I'm talking about your life online. You're at risk of having your computer taken over so that perfect strangers can read your e-mail, access your bank accounts, pilfer your credit card numbers, and even steal your identity.

2 I've seen this over and over again at my summer job as a computer technician at a nationwide computer store. You wouldn't believe how many computers are compromised and infected.

3 As college students, we're particularly vulnerable because we spend so much time online. According to David Tatar, manager of Wisconsin's Consumer Office of Privacy Protection, 32 percent of all identity theft claims are filed by people between the ages of 18 and 29 years old. That's the largest percentage of any age group.

4 Today I'd like to explain three additional steps that experts recommend for online security—using strong passwords, using secure connections, and double-checking links before clicking on them.

5 Step 1: The first step is using strong passwords—for e-mail accounts, bank accounts, and everything else that you do online. What makes a strong password? Take a look at this example: IwbiP;;4387-CSamFF. Now this is a long password, but that is part of its strength. The first criterion of a strong password is having 10 characters; 15 or more is even better—like the one I showed you. It should also include upper- and lowercase letters, numbers, and punctuation such as semicolons, hyphens, and underscores.

6 According to Microsoft's online guide to creating strong passwords, when your passwords contain long combinations of seemingly random letters, numbers, and punctuation, your security increases exponentially—meaning that a password like the one I showed you is literally billions of times more secure than something short and ordinary like *hot dog* or *college*.

7 In addition to having a strong password, you should use a secure connection whenever possible. How do you know if a connection is secure or insecure? Here's an insecure connection. If you look at the address bar, you'll see the first letters are *http*—highlighted here with the red arrow. Whenever you see *http* in a Web site address, your connection is not secure. It's fine to read Web sites with this kind of connection, but you should never transmit sensitive information over *http*. When the connection is secure, it will begin with *https*—as in this example. And think of the "s" as standing for "safe" or "secure."

8 So far we've seen the importance of having a strong password and of using secure connections whenever transmitting sensitive data. The third step is double-checking links before you click them. This is a little more involved than the previous steps, but it's just as important.

9 For example, here is an e-mail that was supposedly sent from my bank, Franklin Bank. It tells me that I need to click on the blue link in order to

update my account information. But if we take a closer look, we can see that while the link says *BankFranklin.com*, the actual destination is another site entirely. If I hold my cursor over the link for a second or two without clicking on it, the yellow box that pops up will show the real Web site—not Franklin Bank, but something called *ssedu.org.cn/dede*.

10   This looks like it might be my bank's information, but it's not. It's a fraudulent Web site run by a hacker who's trying to gain access to my financial information. By double-checking potentially questionable links before you click on them, you can avoid scams like this one.

11   What do you do if the e-mail link doesn't match the one your cursor reveals? The answer is: Don't click—it's as simple as that.

12   At the beginning of this speech, I said that you're at risk, and that's true. But you're not helpless. I've shared three proven ways to protect yourself—strong passwords, secure connections, and double-checking links. I hope you'll find this information helpful as you fight this endless battle for online security.

D.   Main issues/chapters covered in the course.

Main Issues/Chapters

- Selecting a Topic and a Purpose
- Analyzing the Audience
- Supporting Your Ideas
- Organizing and Outlining
  Organizing the Body of the Speech
  Beginning and Ending the Speech
  Outlining the Speech
- Using language
- Delivering the Speech
- Using Visual Aids
- Speaking to Inform
- Speaking to Persuade
- Speaking on Special Occasions

In-Class Procedure

PPT/Directions	活动过程描述
Pre-Class Assignment	**课前任务**
2. Can you imagine what kind of speech American students produce? Better than yours? Or worse? Curious? American student's English speech full of faults? Can't believe it? Watch the video and find out!	1. 这项活动旨在使学生在学期初通过实例分析，了解英语演讲课程的主要教学内容。 2. 学期第一次课结束时，播放《演讲的艺术教师用书》随书赠送的DVD中美国学生的演讲视频"Securing Yourself Online (Need-Improvement Version)"。告知学生，演讲存在不足，需要改进。 A. 播放完第一遍，请学生与周围同学进行一分钟讨论，讨论自己对视频的感觉。 B. 再播放一遍。 C. 要求学生课后仔细阅读演讲稿，并多次观看演讲视频。要求每位学生找出演讲中至少五点不足。学生离开教室之前应领取一份演讲稿复印件；视频（只放需要修改的版本）应放在网络平台，供所有学生下载或观看。 （六分钟。）
In-Class Procedure	**课堂活动描述**
3–5 Group discussion: What's wrong exactly? • Ideas… • Organization… • Language… • Delivery… … 6. Class report: Let's list the problems. No. 1 … No. 2 … No. 3 … … No repetitions!	3. 第一次课时，将60人的大班分为12个小组，五人一个小组，并编号，以便本学期的各种小组讨论。 4. 将两分钟的视频再播放一次，帮助学生刷新记忆。学生手中应有讲稿，以便随时参照和做笔记。本节课的整个活动都要求学生随时参照演讲稿。 5. 小组讨论。汇总组员们找出的问题，需要做简单的笔记。提醒各小组，讨论结束后，需要有一名代表发言。 （五分钟。） 6. 班级汇报。各小组汇报讨论结果，每组不得超过一分钟。要求：第一，需要对问题进行编号，如：First… Second…；第二，从第二小组开始，不得重复已经被说过的内容。 （这个环节计划12分钟，但因为越往后，可以补充的新内容会越少，因此实际比计划时间短。） 到后面几组发言时，教师可给予适当提示。学生很可能没有找出所有的问题，但他们在稍后与最终版本对比后，会有更大收获。

（待续）

PPT/Directions	活动过程描述
7. Group discussion: Watch the final version and compare. 	Final	vs.	Need-Improvement
---	---	---
…	vs.	…
…	vs.	…
…	vs.	…
…	vs.	…
…		…		7. 播放修改后的版本（参见 Materials/Preparation C）。提醒学生：仍然是那个学生，仍然是那个题目，但前后的对比更暴露出第一个版本的问题。 观看完毕，小组自由讨论五分钟。要求找出第二个版本和第一个版本之间的差别。注意做笔记，并对主要论点进行编号。 （10分钟。）
8. Class Report (≤one min.) New Discoveries?	8. 讨论完毕，小组汇报。仍遵循上一场汇报时的规则，但需要从第12组开始。 学生需要回答：演讲人在第一个版本中的哪些不足，在最终版中以怎样的方式得以解决？当然，学生通过对比，可能发现之前未发现的新的问题。（可参考 Materials/Preparation B 的分析）。 （10分钟。）
9–10 English public speaking is *not just English*! Public speaking skills are improved! ↓ What to learn in the course?	9. 班级讨论完毕，教师将案例中的细节问题系统化。对比分析之后，学生应了解到，通过系统学习，自己可以达到什么标准。 10. 以此展开，向学生介绍这门课所要学习的主要内容（参见 Materials/Preparation D）。除了最后两项之外，所有内容均在案例分析中有较深入的讨论。 此后，在每一章学习过程中，都可提醒学生回忆这两个版本之间差别，以加深记忆。 （五分钟。）

Comments/Reflections

1. Determine what's wrong with the original version (the need-improvement version) of an American student's speech and find out solutions from his final version. Such exercise not only is used as a stimulus to group and class discussion, but also presents to students a vivid picture of what a good public speech is like and what they can achieve within the duration of this course. As stated previously, this activity is better arranged at the beginning of the semester to present a broad picture about the course.

2. Students would be very much excited to see that an average American student can also make an awkward and embarrassing speech, as they may previously have a misconception that English public

speaking is just about English. They will see how much they are to learn and achieve beyond the English language. The activity shows them, instead of telling them, that the course deserves their time and effort.

3. A frequent challenge for the instructor of a big class of 60 students is how to engage students in class activities while having good time management. There are two things here to share with instructors.

    The first is preparation—help students get fully prepared for group discussion. It is almost predictable that group discussion would be a failure if students were only allowed to watch the two video clips once in class—even if most students succeeded struggling to get the main point, it is not enough for them to make much commitment to the discussion. To make sure they have something to say, first make them fully understand the original version. Give them time to prepare before class.

    The second is good control of students' speaking time. It's a bit tricky, but the less students are able to produce, the less speaking time should be allowed for them.

本活动的设计受到以下文献的启发：Schneider, Valerie. (1995). Pointers for Polished Public Speaking. In Lucas, Stephen E. (ed.) *Selections from the Speech Communication Teacher, 1991–1994*. Madison, Wisconsin: McGraw-Hill. 10–11.

Goal: To provide an opportunity for students to showcase their public speaking skills developed during the basic speech course.

Class Size: 100 students.

Time: Preparation + 90 mins.

Pre-Class Reading Assignment: None.

Materials/Preparation: A. Judges' guide and ballot.

Judges' Guide and Ballot	
Participant's Number: Total Score (230 points):	
Introduction	
1. Gained attention and interest (10 points)	
2. Introduced topic clearly (10 points)	
3. Established credibility (10 points)	
4. Previewed body of speech (10 points)	
5. Related to audience (10 points)	
Body	
6. Main points clear (10 points)	
7. Main points fully supported (10 points)	
8. Organization well planned (10 points)	
9. Language accurate (10 points)	
10. Language clear and concise (10 points)	
11. Language appropriate (10 points)	
12. Connectives effective (10 points)	
Conclusion	
13. Prepared audience for ending (10 points)	
14. Reinforced central idea (10 points)	
Delivery	
15. Maintained strong eye contact (10 points)	

（待续）

Judges' Guide and Ballot	
16. Used voice effectively (10 points)	
17. Pronunciation clear (10 points)	
18. Used physical actions effectively (10 points)	
19. Presented visual aids well (10 points)	
Overall Evaluation	
20. Topic challenging (10 points)	
21. Specific purpose well chosen (10 points)	
22. Message adapted to audience (10 points)	
23. Speech completed within time limit (10 points)	

B. Awards for the winners:

First Prize

Second Prize

Third Prize

Best Pronunciation

…

In-Class Procedure

PPT/Directions	活动过程描述
Preparation	**演讲比赛准备**
1. The Outstanding Speaker Contest • The last week of the term Specially Designed for the Course!	1. 开学第一次课进行课程介绍时，向学生说明学期末将安排一场演讲比赛。比赛有别于一般的口语大赛，将考查学生对公众演讲知识以及演讲技能的掌握情况。参加演讲比赛的同学可以免去期末演讲考试。（演讲比赛参与者和获奖者获得一定奖励，以学分或奖品的方式。）
2–3 Chance for Everybody! • Not just pronunciation! • 23 items (All covered in the course.) • Enough time to prepare • Three-minute speech Ready?	2. 比赛形式为有准备的自选题目演讲，演讲时间为三分钟。 比赛是为了鼓励学生扎扎实实地实践课堂上学习的理论知识。要求学生在一个学期的几次实践中，至少有一次演讲体现出受过正规的训练。同时，比赛规则使得比赛不会限定在几个语音漂亮的学生中间，而是鼓励所有学生都参与。 3. 100人的班级分为20个小组，小组不宜过大（每个小组不超过五人），以便活动时充分讨论。学期末将由每个小组推选一位学生参加比赛。

（待续）

PPT/Directions	活动过程描述
4. Judges' Ballot (23 items) Introduction … Body … Conclusion … Delivery … Overall Evaluation … These are what you are to learn!	4. Materials/Preparation 所提供的评分表非常重要。这份评分表可以囊括演讲课所学的重要内容。因此，在平时上课进行演讲分析时，这份评分表几乎每次都用。在没有系统学习理论知识时，学生可以根据自己的感受打分；而在相关各章的学习完成后，则需根据原则来评估。 这份评分表说明，仅有漂亮的语音是不够的，因为发音只占了其中的一项。同时，均衡地将分值分配到每一项，是为了强调，每一章节的知识都是重要的。这样的评分制度向所有认真学习的学生倾斜。 这种处理方法背后的理念是：学生只有掌握系统的演讲知识后，才能得到显著提高。
5–7 Preliminary Contests ↓ • Select the speaker of the group. • Prepare for the final.	5. 在学期的倒数第三或第四周，安排20分钟时间，在小组内先进行比赛，然后确定一位参赛选手。小组的比赛规则可由小组自定。 6. 准备期间，小组成员有责任帮助参赛选手，包括演讲稿的修改及建议、操练指导等。（全学期的小组协作可以作为平时成绩的一部分考虑。） 7. 比赛的组织工作可交给班干部，包括安排主持人、工作人员及各项流程。
Contest	**演讲比赛**
8–11 The Final Competition • Everybody has a say. • Everybody is the judge. Find the best trained speaker!	8. 评委。评委由班上的学生担任，一个小组将提交一份评分表。按照以往的经验，一位学生在三分钟内打出23项分数比较困难，因此比赛中小组成员需要分配评分表中的项目，当然最后也可以在一起商量决定某些项目。一般情况下，每一项都需要打分，如果选手有一项没有体现出来（例如，没有preview），那么，该项即为0分。 9. 教师的责任：保证比赛程序顺利进行。 10. 每位选手演讲完毕，留出半分钟至一分钟时间收集评分表。中场可以稍作休息。 11. 颁奖；教师简单点评。

1. There is every good reason for the instructor of a big class of 100 students or over to arrange a public speaking contest toward the end of the semester. Hopefully a bigger event can be held if there are parallel classes. It provides students with an opportunity to showcase their public speaking skills and at the same time stimulates all students to work hard.

2. The key to the contest is to make sure that everybody has a hand in it and that equal chances are created for everybody.

3. This outstanding speaker contest here is different in nature from other speaking contests that we are familiar with. It is so designed as to check whether students have had a good command of what was learned during the semester. Common misunderstandings among students include ideas that public speaking skills are born, or are just based on presentation skills, or are decided by one's oral English. With these misconceptions, students can't grasp the essence of public speaking, especially when as a part of rhetoric.

4. The judges' ballot (or used as the evaluation form in class) makes it clear that the winners are expected to have really learned what they should have about public speaking. It is vital to have all the 23 items equally measured in order to encourage students to learn every part of the theories and put them into practice.

5. Students are to make a prepared speech instead of an impromptu speech, because during the preparation students will have a chance to apply all the theories into practice—choosing a topic, deciding the purpose and the central idea, outlining, finding supporting details, polishing language... This is what we want. And this is the only way average students can really improve.

本活动的设计受到以下文献的启发：Rifkind, Lawrence. (1995). The Outstanding Speaker Contest. In Lucas, Stephen E. (ed.) *Selections from the Speech Communication Teacher, 1991–1994*. Madison, Wisconsin: McGraw-Hill. 53–54.

PART 2

Preparation and Presentation—General

Speech Anxiety

UNDERSTANDING TEACHING

The human brain starts working the moment you are born and never stops until you stand up to speak in public.

—Sir George Jessel

I would be loath to cast away my speech, for besides that it is excellently well penned, I have taken great pains to con it.

—Shakespeare

TEACHER'S GUIDE (Q & A)

➤ **为什么会产生演讲焦虑?**

在演讲课堂与实际生活中，人们只要在公众场合下发表自己的看法与观点，或在公众场合下演讲，绝大多数人都会觉得紧张焦虑。要想克服这种紧张焦虑情绪，我们首先必须了解引起焦虑的原因：

- 完美主义者，怕出错；
- 太在意听众的看法；
- 恐"高"，就是面对的听众比自己的地位高或懂得多、听众人数过大时有压力；
- 不习惯当众说话；
- 准备不充分；
- 身体状况不佳。

➤ **如何有效地应对演讲焦虑?**

- 学会调整心态；
- 演讲者应认识到紧张感是演讲中的一种自然现象；
- 积累公众演讲的经验；
- 掌握上台前缓解紧张情绪的方法；
- 充分准备；
- 保持良好的身体状况；
- 谈论自己熟悉的内容与话题。

> ### 该教学环节何时进行？

在《演讲的艺术》第十版（中国版）教材中，该环节集中安排在第二章"演讲的自信心与道德观"(Speaking Confidently and Ethically, *APS*, Chapter 2, pp. 16–23)中，也就是学完演讲的基本要素与理论后，因此本教学环节可以安排在第二次课上。在讲解完演讲的历史与重要性后，就可以进行本教学环节的内容。

> ### 该教学环节有何必要性？

演讲课程是一门需要学生不断参与与展示自己的课程，通过本教学环节的讲解，可以让学生了解到为什么在演讲时会紧张，如何处理自己在演讲时的紧张情绪，因此本教学环节十分重要。

> ### 常见的教学困难

- 性格内向的学生尤其不愿意在公众场合下讲话。在实际教学中，教师要有足够的耐心与学生交流，取得学生的信任。这是顺利开展活动的第一步。
- 学生往往不愿意成为第一位上场或展示的人，教师应予以鼓励，甚至可以以奖励期末考核分数的方式，"重赏之下必有勇夫"。

> ### 教与学的误区

- 大多数学生认为演讲是讲究个人天赋的，对演讲心存畏惧。演讲是一项可以通过训练获得提高的技能。演讲中的焦虑与紧张并不是不可克服的，也不是与生俱来的。
- 很多学生认为只要有充分的准备就一定能够克服演讲中的焦虑与紧张。实际上，仅仅靠准备是不够的。演讲是一个动态的变化的过程，演讲者无法预测演讲过程中会发生什么，演讲结束后会怎么样。准备充分能够有效地缓解紧张与焦虑，但还要辅以其他方法，如演讲中随时注意听众的反应、进行适当的调整等。正如有些学者所说："最好的演讲不是严格按照准备来进行的演讲，也不是完全不准备的演讲，而是有充分准备并且准备随时调整的演讲。"
- 认为演讲技巧可以依靠背诵几篇演讲稿，或者观看几篇经典的演讲视频就能够提高。实际上，演讲有系统的科学的训练体系，只有按规律训练、学习，才能在演讲的时候更自信，让自己的演讲更吸引人。

7.1

It's Not Necessary to Be Nervous If I Can Do These

Goal: To introduce some skills to students for them to deal with nervousness.

Class Size: Any.

Time: 25–30 mins.

Pre-Class Reading Assignment: Speaking Confidently and Ethically (*APS*, Chapter 2, pp. 16–23).

Materials/Preparation: Two groups of Chinese poems: simple and familiar vs. challenging and less familiar.

Simple Chinese Poems

七步诗	敕勒歌	咏鹅	静夜思
曹植	北朝民歌	骆宾王	李白
煮豆持作羹,	敕勒川,	鹅，鹅，鹅,	床前明月光,
漉菽以为汁。	阴山下。	曲项向天歌。	疑是地上霜。
萁在釜下燃,	天似穹庐,	白毛浮绿水,	举头望明月,
豆在釜中泣,	笼盖四野。	红掌拨清波。	低头思故乡。
本是同根生,	天苍苍, 野茫茫,		
相煎何太急?	风吹草低见牛羊。		

Difficult Chinese Poems

蒹葭	涉江采芙蓉	望月怀远	寄李亿员外
《诗经》	《古诗十九首》	张九龄	鱼玄机
蒹葭苍苍,	涉江采芙蓉,	海上生明月,	羞日遮罗袖,
白露为霜。	兰泽多芳草。	天涯共此时。	愁春懒起妆。
所谓伊人,	采之欲遗谁,	情人怨遥夜,	易求无价宝,
在水一方。	所思在远道。	竟夕起相思。	难得有情郎。
溯洄从之,	还顾望旧乡,	灭烛怜光满,	枕上潜垂泪,
道阻且长;	长路漫浩浩。	披衣觉露滋。	花间暗断肠。
溯游从之,	同心而离居,	不堪盈手赠,	自能窥宋玉,
宛在水中央。	忧伤以终老。	还寝梦佳期。	何必恨王昌?

PPT/Directions	活动过程描述
1. The first round Volunteer to recite Chinese poems with 30 seconds' preparation.	1. 教师在全班寻求一位自愿者，上台背诵两首中国古诗词。可以选择一位平时比较活跃的学生，或者语文比较好的学生，来确定自愿者。在正式背诵之前，自愿者将会有30秒钟的准备时间。
2. Prepare the first poem (30 seconds). **七步诗** 曹植 煮豆持作羹， 漉菽以为汁。 萁在釜下燃， 豆在釜中泣， 本是同根生， 相煎何太急？	2. 让该学生读第一首诗（参见 Materials/Preparation），30秒钟准备时间后背诵。
3–4 Recite the poem.	3. 30秒钟后，教师提醒自愿者时间到，邀请自愿者面向全班同学，开始背诵诗词。 4. 背完后，教师用一两句话简要评价自愿者的背诵。
5. Prepare the second poem (30 seconds). **蒹葭** 《诗经》 蒹葭苍苍， 白露为霜。 所谓伊人， 在水一方。 溯洄从之， 道阻且长； 溯游从之， 宛在水中央。	5. 教师展示第二首诗词（参见 Materials/Preparation），同样有30秒钟的准备时间。

（待续）

PPT/Directions	活动过程描述
6. Recite the poem.	6. 教师计时，时间到后，邀请自愿者面向全班同学，开始背诵诗词。
7. The next round of the game.	7. 选择下一位同学继续进行该活动，规则同上。 如果没有自愿者，可以由上一位自愿者在全班随意指定一位同学。规则同上。
8–9 Interview the students: What is his or her feeling when reading the first poem? How about the second one? And explain why. The Importance of the Experience ↓ Speech Anxiety	8. 多轮背诵后，教师邀请两位参与背诵的同学上场，采访他们在背诵两首诗时的心理状态。 9. 进入课堂讲解环节，如何处理演讲中的紧张情绪。

Comments/Reflections

1. Most students find this activity interesting. At the beginning, the participants may be a little nervous knowing what poem he or she is going to recite. However, after the first poem, the participant will be more eager to try the second. But, when the poem is revealed—longer and more difficult, most of them will be nervous again. The biggest challenge for them is not to have enough time to prepare. This activity will make students understand the importance of preparation for a successful speech.

2. The duration of the activity can be decided by the instructor. It could be more than two rounds. Honestly speaking, two rounds will be fine since students will refuse to continue the game due to the difficulty of the second poem. Anyway, two rounds will be enough for them to learn a lesson.

Public Speaking: Reducing Anxiety and Revealing a Process

Goal: To help students overcome communication anxiety and simultaneously gain an overview of the public speaking process.

Class Size: Any.

Time: 25–30 mins.

Pre-Class Reading Assignment: Supporting Your Ideas (*APS*, Chapter 6, pp. 72–83).

Materials/Preparation: None.

🕐 In-Class Procedure

PPT/Directions	活动过程描述
Pre-Class Assignment	**课前任务**
Prepare for the interview. • Topic • Questions	教师要求学生课前准备一些采访的问题，用来采访其搭档。采访的话题可以是学生对搭档感兴趣的某个主题，比如怎么克服困难实现某个目标，或者生活的某个转折。采访时间为五分钟。
In-Class Procedure	**课堂活动过程**
1–2 The first round of interview.	1. 学生利用课前任务中准备的问题访谈自己的搭档。（五分钟） 教师要求访谈时，采访者必须做笔记，记录受访者的一些重要信息。 2. 教师计时。同时，教师在教室来回走动，确保所有学生都能够参与到访谈中，并且提醒采访者记笔记。
3. The second round of interview.	3. 访谈结束后，访谈双方进行角色互换。开始新一轮的访谈，规则与时间同第一轮访谈一样。
4. Prepare the outline of your speech.	4. 第二轮访谈结束后，每位同学将在访谈中获得的信息整理成一篇课堂小演讲的大纲。（五分钟。）
5. Present your speech.	5. 五分钟后，教师将会邀请五位同学，他们将在全班同学面前介绍所获得的他们搭档的信息。每位同学的演讲时间为三分钟。

（待续）

PPT/Directions	活动过程描述
6–7 Comments and conclusion.	6. 在每一位同学演讲完后，教师邀请该演讲者的搭档简述演讲者介绍的是否属实，有无重要信息缺失。 7. 最后对五位同学的演讲分别进行点评与总结。

Comments/Reflections

1. This activity helps students develop their abilities to gather and tailor information, as well as improve their note-taking skills. It also helps students understand that preparation is very important for them to reduce speech anxiety.

2. During the activity, the instructor can also encourage students to use other methods to enhance their confidence, like thinking positively, regarding speaking as an opportunity to share your ideas with others and to practice speaking skills, etc.

Goal:	To know ways of dealing with speech anxiety and practice making a short speech.
Class size:	30 students.
Time:	30 mins.
Pre-Class Reading Assignment:	Speaking Confidently and Ethically (*APS*, Chapter 2, pp. 16–23).
Materials/Preparation:	A. A video clip about ways of handling speech anxiety (available on http://heep. unipus. cn).
	B. Questions on the video clip.

Questions on the Video Clip

1. As Step 1, what would you visualize to help reduce speech anxiety? What kinds of mental images do athletes usually have before they take competition?
2. As Step 2, what would you drink to reduce speech anxiety and why?
3. As Step 3, what would you do and what would you visualize to handle the stage fright?
4. As Step 4, what would you imagine related to the audience?
5. As Step 5, why should you focus on one thing before making a speech?
6. As Step 6, what would you do to release pressure?
7. As Step 7, what would you bring with you when you are going to speak?
8. As Step 8, why would reading poems help you make a better speech?

In-Class Procedure

PPT/Directions	活动过程描述
1. • Do you have speech anxiety when you make speeches? Explain why or why not. • Do you have such experiences when speaking in public: shaking, sweating, and having butterflies in your stomach, dry mouth, rapid heartbeat, and squeaky voice? Explain why or why not.	1. 教师在PPT上展示几个要求学生思考的问题，学生可以写下自己想法的关键词。（一分钟。） 2. 请两位同学向全班同学分享自己的答案。要求学生不仅说出答案，而且要解释原因。每位同学的发言时间为一分钟。

（待续）

PPT/Directions	活动过程描述
3. Critical thinking: What kinds of approaches have you adopted to handle speech anxiety?	3. Pair work：讨论哪些方法可以解决演讲过程中的焦虑？讨论时记下要点。（五分钟）
4. Share your experience.	4. 教师邀请两到三位同学向全班同学分享他们处理演讲焦虑的经验。每位同学的演讲时间为两分钟。
5. Watch the video clip twice. • For the first time, watch the video and take notes. • For the second time, watch the video and think about the questions.	5. 播放视频短片（参见 Materials/Preparation A）： • 在第一次观看视频短片时，教师要求学生边看视频边记笔记。 • 在第二次观看短片时，教师向学生展示 Materials/Preparation B 中的问题，让学生先熟悉这些问题，希望他们看完视频后能够回答这些问题。
6. Questions: 1) How many methods were mentioned in the video to deal with speech anxiety? 2) Which method would you prefer to use and why?	6. 问学生在视频中共谈到了几种处理紧张情绪的方法，哪种方法是他们最喜欢的，并解释为什么。
7–9 • Practice your favorite approach. • One-minute introductory speech.	7. 要求学生准备一篇一分钟的介绍性演讲，可以介绍自己的老师、朋友、同学等自己比较熟悉的人。 8. 请同学在全班面前演讲，希望能够用到已经学过的处理紧张情绪的方法。 9. 活动结束后，教师将对学生的演讲进行评价，主要针对处理紧张情绪方面。
10. Summary: How to deal with speech anxiety.	10. 教师系统讲述如何克服演讲中的紧张情绪。

Comments/Reflections

1. This activity is designed for students to discuss the ways of handling speech anxiety. The video helps students practice listening, speaking and taking notes as well.

2. The video, which lasts less than three minutes, is applicable in class; it is so humorous as to arouse students' interest to explore it and follow some suggestions accordingly.

3. This activity may start with warm-up exercises: Talk about your own experience with speech anxiety or stage fright, and the methods you have used to overcome them. Then, pair work or group discussion may be organized after the video is played.

(供稿人：郭建 中国科学院大学；改编人：周红兵)

Communication Awareness

UNDERSTANDING TEACHING

He that converses not knows nothing.

—A Proverb

Public speaking professionals say that you win or lose the battle to hold your audience in the first 30 seconds of a given presentation.

—John Medina

TEACHER'S GUIDE (Q & A)

➤ **什么是交流意识?**

- 广义地说，"意识"可以指人们对事物或环境的感知、洞察以及积极而恰当地做出反应的能力。因此，"交流意识"可以涵盖对交流目的以及交流过程中各参与者的感知、洞察以及应对的能力。公众演讲作为一种交流艺术，演讲者在演讲过程中自身的表现以及对公众做出的反应均体现其交流意识水平。

- 本章的"交流意识"有所侧重，主要针对中国学生在公众演讲中存在的突出问题，强调对演讲目的以及听众身份的"意识"。通俗地讲，演讲者应该始终牢记演讲要达到的交流效果，始终清楚自己的演讲对象。

➤ **该教学环节何时进行?**

- 这一环节不一定集中讲授，但每节课都会涉及到。

- "交流意识"是公众演讲的基础与核心，贯穿课程的所有主要章节。可以从三个方面理解。

- 首先，只要是信息交流，必然有交流目的。在《演讲的艺术》第十版（中国版）教材中，主要章节均突显对交流目的的要求。例如：
  A. 在演讲准备阶段，首先需要确定演讲目的（selecting a purpose）；
  B. 从交流目的出发，演讲大致可分为"信息性演讲（informative speech）"和"说服性演讲（persuasive speech）"；

C. "特殊场合演讲（speech for special occasions）"更要求满足特定场合的交流目的等等。

因此，在这些章节的讲授中，教师首先应该关注，学生演讲时是否始终清楚自己演讲的信息交流目的。

- 其次，交流目的的实现依赖于对交流过程各环节的正确处理，其关键落在"听众分析（audience analysis）"上。"听众分析"渗透在演讲的各个环节，从选题、立意、布局到语言使用、舞台呈现等方面均要求演讲者清楚地意识到听众对象的存在。

- 最后，舞台演讲（delivery）中，交流意识特别表现在演讲者与听众保持视线交流（eye contact），关注听众的反应，灵活应对；必要时，可能需要做出临场的调整。

➤ **如何帮助学生提升交流意识？**

- 首先，提醒并检查学生在演讲时能否时刻关注交流目的。例如，信息性演讲是否最终达到成功传递意向信息的目的？说服性演讲是否最终对听众产生了意向中的影响？

- 教师可以做这样的检验：在学生的有备演讲结束时，再次提问学生的演讲目的，检查学生是否回答时表现犹豫，是否给出与自己提纲中相左的演讲目的（这种情况下，学生应该提前完成提纲和讲稿写作）。

- 其次，请听众同学协助，从他们的角度（或假设听众群的角度），对演讲的选题、主题、价值取向、语言风格、舞台风格等各环节进行审视、批判和建议。

- 在听众意识方面，尤其应该关注跨文化交际的内容。

➤ **常见的教学困难**

教学的主要困难有两点：

第一，用英语进行演讲的要求使得学生过多地关注英语语言表达，而忽视了真正的交流目的。

第二，学生过多地关注自己的表演，而忽视了听众的兴趣与获得感。

➤ **教与学的误区**

- 师生双方均缺乏真实的交流意识，误以为：英语演讲的首要目的是"秀"英语；听众也主要以英语水平来评价演讲水平，因此，英语演讲的成败关键是英语讲得好不好。

- 学生随意选题，教师亦重视不够，导致演讲的交流目的一开始就不真实，因而也不明确，导致演讲中途迷失方向。

- 学生在准备过程中未能充分考虑听众的背景和需求。

- 学生对跨文化交际的理解狭窄或关注不够，包括中西文化之间的差异以及不同社会、文化群体之间的认知差异。

8.1 How to Maintain the Audience's Interest During Your Speech

Goal: To help students improve the ability to analyze the audience's feedback, and then respond to the audience appropriately.

Class Size: 25–30 students.

Time: 30–35 mins.

Pre-Class Reading Assignment: Delivering the Speech (*APS*, Chapter 11, pp. 146–158).

Materials/Preparation: Question cards.

Question Card 1

During your speech, you find that some of the audience begin to leave one by one. How would you respond?

Question Card 2

When you are speaking, you find that some of the audience are whistling, and some are shouting. How would you respond?

Question Card 3

During your speech, you find that it is the right time for dinner. How would you respond?

Question Card 4

During your speech, you find that some of the audience are sleeping or murmuring with each other. How would you respond?

PPT/Directions	活动过程描述
Pre-Class Assignment	**课前任务**
• Two-minute speech. • The most interesting thing in my life.	准备一个关于"人生中最有趣的一件事"的演讲。演讲时间为两分钟。
In-Class Procedure	**课堂活动描述**
1–3 Speech of Group 1.	1. 把学生分成四组，每组人数不能少于六人，具体分组方法视全班人数而定。 2. 教师随机从第一组中邀请一位同学向全班作关于人生中最有趣的一件事的演讲。演讲时间为两分钟。 3. 在听第一组某位同学演讲时，第二组全体组员在该同学演讲时一个接一个纷纷离场。
4. Speech of Group 2.	4. 第二组的代表上台开始演讲。第三组人员在听第二组某位同学演讲时，制造各种噪音，如吹口哨、尖叫等。
5. Speech of Group 3.	5. 第三组的代表上台开始演讲。第四组的同学在听第三组某位同学演讲时，做出到了吃饭时间很饿、不耐烦、着急要走的样子。
6. Speech of Group 4.	6. 第四组的代表上台演讲。在听第四组的同学演讲时，第一组同学假装要睡觉或几个人小声地窃窃私语。
7–8 Group discussion.	7. 所有小组代表演讲结束后，教师向每个小组发一张问题卡（参见 Materials/Preparation），每组讨论的问题就是该组代表在演讲中遇到的问题。 8. 小组讨论该组代表在演讲时是否合理地处理了该问题，并提出更多解决该问题的方法。
9. Group reflection.	9. 教师最后请每个小组派一位代表（最好不是开始的演讲者）向全班介绍如何处理演讲中碰到的那些问题。
10. Comments.	10. 教师总结本次课程，并给学生一些指导性建议或方法。

Comments/Reflections

1. This activity helps students understand the importance of communication awareness in public speaking, especially when they are the speakers. It will also help students improve skills in analyzing audience feedback during the speech.

2. One problem in practicing this activity is how to encourage the audience to embarrass the speaker by causing trouble in various ways, because they would think it is impolite to do so. Some would even feel guilty when the speaker finally gives up because he or she is not able to handle the situation. However, all the students will learn a lesson on ethical listening as well as ethical speaking.

Goal:	To identify and engage the elements of the interpersonal communication process.
Class Size:	Any.
Time:	20–25 mins.
Pre-Class Reading Assignment:	Using Language (*APS*, Chapter 10, pp. 130–144); Using Visual Aids (*APS*, Chapter 12, pp. 160–175).
Materials/Preparation:	15 blank index cards with a word on each of them. Suggested words for each round: Round 1: pencil, tree, football, flower, baseball bat, chair. Round 2: building, screw-driver, cat, airplane, car. Round 3: house, hammer, person, television, mouse.

🕐 In-Class Procedure

PPT/Directions	活动过程描述
1–6 **General Rules** • Message Sender; Message Receiver. • Sender gets a card with a word on it. • Sender gives verbal clues to Receiver. • Sender can't give that word directly. • Receiver draws a picture of the word. • Receivre pronounces the word.	1. 教师首先将学生分成二至五组，每组三至六位学生。每组都将会有三个回合的游戏。 2. 在每一回合的游戏中，每组会选择一位同学出来接收信息，其他的组员全部为信息发出者，发送信息时必须按照要求发送。 3. 教师在学生明确自己的角色后，将给每个小组的信息发送者发放一张卡片，不准让接收者与其他小组的人员看见卡片内容。每张卡片只能使用一次，不可重复使用。 4. 当信息发送者接收到自己的任务卡片上的单词时，他们只可以使用语言来告诉接收者关于该单词的信息。 5. 信息接收者（不能看信息发送者，即说话者）将尽力根据自己听到的为线索，在黑板上画出该单词表示的事物。 6. 每组每个回合的活动时间均为两分钟。

（待续）

PPT/Directions	活动过程描述
7. Rules for Round 1 • No questions. • No eye contact. • No communication at all. • No corrections.	7. 第一回合的其他规则：信息接收者只能够通过听的方式来获取信息。不能提出问题，也不能修改自己的答案，更不能看信息发送者。
8. Rule for Round 2 • Same as above. • Only corrections allowed.	8. 第二回合的其他规则：条件大致与第一回合相同，但是在第二回合，信息接收者可以修改自己的答案，但仍然不能提问，也不能看信息发送者。
9. Rules for Round 3 • All communication allowed. • Corrections allowed.	9. 第三回合的其他规则：此回合，信息接受者可以与信息发送者有语言与非语言的交际，可以面对信息发送者，也可以在游戏结束前的任何时候来修改自己的答案。
10. • Who's the winner? • Claim your prize.	10. 授课教师每个回合给每小组积分，积分规则为：信息接收者猜对卡片上的信息则获得一分，猜错则不加分。如果猜错了，其他组可以抢猜答案，抢猜对了的小组，可以获得一分。 11. 三轮游戏结束后，分数最高的组为获胜组。 12. 获胜的小组可以获得教师的奖品，或奖励平时成绩分数。具体由授课教师自己取舍。

Comments/Reflections

1. This activity can make students have a vivid understanding about three different views of communication: the linear view of communication by showing a one-directional approach of communication, the interactive view of communication by allowing for the inclusion of limited feedback, and the transitive view of communication by showing that people can act as both senders and receivers within communication contexts.

2. This activity helps students use different ways to speak or convey the information to the audience in a more effective way according to the audience's feedback.

本活动的设计来源于以下文献：Lippert, Lance & Paynton, Scott T. (2001). Send, Receive, and Draw. In Lucas, Stephen E. (ed.) *Selections from the Speech Communication Teacher, 1996–1999*. Madison, Wisconsin: McGraw-Hill. 98–101.

Audience Analysis

UNDERSTANDING TEACHING

Culture is the collective programming of the mind that distinguishes the members of one category of people from another.

—Geert Hofstede

If you talk to a man in a language he understands, that goes to his head. If you talk to him in his language, that goes to his heart.

—Nelson Mandela

TEACHER'S GUIDE (Q & A)

➤ **学完听众分析后，学生能够掌握什么?**

- 能够解释为什么演讲者要以听众为中心。
- 能够解释听众以自我为中心所指的是什么。
- 能够有效地识别听众的人文特征。
- 能够有效地识别听众的场景特征。
- 能够使用问卷调查为自己的演讲进行听众分析。

➤ **什么是以听众为中心?**

- 出色的演讲者都是以听众为中心的，因为演讲的基本目的是要从听众那里赢得预期的反应与效果。所谓的以听众为中心并不是一味地为了得到良好的反应而将自己的信念打折扣，甚至改变，也不意味着用超常规的、不正常的、不道德的手段来达到自己的目的。要做到以听众为中心，演讲者就必须知道如何回答下面的问题：
  - 我讲话的听众是谁?
  - 我希望他们在听完我的演讲后了解什么，得到什么，相信什么，或能够做什么?
  - 为了实现或达到自己演讲的目的，演讲者需要用什么样的方式来准备和演示讲稿?

➤ 听众的心理特征主要表现为什么？

一般情况下人都是以自我为中心的，人们只会关注能够影响自己价值观、信仰和切身利益的信息。简单地说，听众会根据自己的认知和意愿来倾听和判断演讲内容。

➤ 如何进行听众分析？

- 确切把握听众的人数。
- 非常了解演讲的场所。
- 密切关注听众的人文特征：性别、年龄、受教育程度、文化背景等。
- 深入了解听众对话题的意向：听众对话题的兴趣、了解程度、态度。
- 了解听众对演讲者所持的态度。
- 了解听众对演讲场合的态度。

➤ 该教学环节在何时进行？

在《演讲的艺术》第十版（中国版）教材中，该环节安排在第五章（Analyzing the Audience, *APS*, Chapter 5, pp. 58–71），在学完演讲的基本要素，进行了第一次课堂演讲后进行。教师在实际教学过程中可以灵活安排自己的教学计划，建议安排在信息性演讲的讲解之前，因为信息性演讲是比较重要的演讲类型，包含话题的选择、材料的准备、讲稿的结构调整，而听众分析是演讲前准备的一个非常重要的环节。

➤ 常见的教学困难

- 学生不知道如何设计一份有效的听众调查问卷，只是简单地模仿其他问卷，设计几个选择题或开放性问答题，也不注重问卷的信度与效度。显然此类问卷浪费人力、物力，对最终的演讲也无很大意义。
- 学生不知道在听众访谈的过程中问什么，以获取更多的听众信息，只是像警察询问笔录一样，问一些关于个人信息的基本问题，不能切中要害，也无法获得对演讲或演讲选题有价值的信息。

➤ 教与学的误区

- 演讲者会错误地以为，只要自己感兴趣的话题，听众一定会感兴趣，从而经常忽略了进行听众分析。
- 一味迎合听众，只要是听众需要的、感兴趣的，演讲者不惜改变自己的想法和价值观。这种演讲容易成为不道德的欺骗性演讲。

Combining Extemporaneous and Impromptu Speaking 9.1

Goal: To provide students with a realistic audience analysis and perspective-taking.

Class Size: Any.

Time: 30 mins.

Pre-Class Reading Assignment: Analyzing the Audience (*APS*, Chapter 5, pp. 58–71).

Materials/Preparation: Sample roles, positions, and audience.

Sample Roles, Positions, and Audience for Students

1. You are an 18-year-old college student in America advocating lowering the drinking age to 18. Your audience consists of members of MADD (Mother Against Drunk Driving).

2. You are a parent who agrees to give your 16-year-old daughter consent to an abortion. The audience is a Catholic Church group oppose to abortion.

3. You are a college student supporting the cancellation of CET–4. Your audience consists of college English teachers and English training school teachers.

4. You are a television producer who defends the program of violent cartoons on Saturday morning. The audience consists of a PTA (Parent-Teacher Association) group attempting to reduce television violence in children's programs.

5. You are a principal defending the necessity of corporal punishment in the junior high school. Your audience consists of parents who are opposed to the use of corporal punishment.

6. You are the city mayor advocating the construction of a new nuclear plant in the city limits. Your audience is a neighborhood group which opposes the construction of a new nuclear plant in their backyard.

7. You are a welfare recipient who is defending the necessity of the current welfare system. Your audience consists of members of a local welfare reform organization.

PPT/Directions	活动过程描述
Pre-Class Assignment	**课前任务**
Prepare for the scenarios: roles, positions and audience.	教师将Materials/Preparation的问题给学生,让学生提前熟悉自己的角色,并根据不同演讲从自己角色出发,提出不同的问题。
In-Class Procedure	**课堂活动描述**
1–4 *Directions:* Every group will recommend a member to be the speaker, while others will be the audience. The speaker will take on the role assigned by the instructor and speak to advocate a particular position.	1. 全班学生分组,每组大概六位学生。 2. 每组推选一位学生,作为本组的演讲者,其他组员则作为演讲者的听众(这里的听众都是持不同意见的听众)。 3. 每组的演讲者将就教师分配的角色来完成一个简短的演讲。演讲时间为五分钟。 4. 所有的角色,都是从教师提前发布给学生的角色中选取的。
6. Group 1 18–year old college student ↓ Mothers Against Drunk Driving	5. 教师开始分配每组的角色,说明每一组演讲者及组员的角色与任务。 6. 第一组 演讲者角色与任务:18岁的美国大学生,倡导并呼吁降低法定饮酒年龄至18岁。 组员的角色与任务:反对酒后驾驶的母亲组织(所有人都是该组织的成员,而且都是母亲,如果你是男生,也要扮成母亲身份)。 7. 分别解释其他组人员的角色。
8. Preparation (five mins.) • State your point. • Define your Point. • Defend your point.	8. 每个小组有五分钟准备时间,演讲者思考如何说服自己的听众接受自己的观点,准备一份半脱稿的开篇演讲,提出自己的观点并予以解释。组员则讨论在问答环节要提出的问题。
9. Speech (five mins.)	9. 准备完后,第一组开始演讲。演讲时间为五分钟。

（待续）

PPT/Directions	活动过程描述
10. Q & A (five mins.)	10. 第一位演讲者结束后，听众开始提问，每位听众的提问时间不能超过15秒。演讲者进行回答。 11. 每组问答时间一共为五分钟。
12. Speech ↓ Audience Analysis	12. 其他小组依次进行。当所有小组的演讲和问答都结束后，教师讲解如何进行听众分析。

Comments/Reflections

1. This activity is a perfect combination of extemporaneous speaking and impromptu speaking. The opening statement is a typical example of an extemporaneous speech, while the Q & A session provides an opportunity for impromptu speaking practice.

2. This activity can also be applied into "Speaking to Persuade" (*APS*, Chapter 14, pp. 192–221). It helps students understand how to persuade the target audience by using some proper language, evidence, and communicative skills.

3. Students will find the activity interesting, taking on the roles they've never played. This to a great extent helps students enhance audience awareness. They will achieve a more tangible understanding about what the audience really need, and how to communicate with them more effectively. One problem with this activity is that most students don't have real experience as a mother of an 18-year-old son or daughter. But they may start to understand true feelings of mothers.

本活动的设计基于以下文献来源：Hazel J. Rozema. (2001). Combining Extemporaneous and Impromptu Speaking. In Lucas, Stephen E. (ed.) *Selections from the Speech Communication Teacher, 1996–1999*. Madison, Wisconsin: McGraw-Hill. 14–15.

9.2   An Alternative to Demographic Audience Analysis

Goal:	To have students differentiate between audience analysis and stereotyping and to have them acquire skills for looking beyond a simplistic demographic analysis so as to enhance their speeches.
Class Size:	30–35 students.
Time:	20–25 mins.
Pre-Class Reading Assignment:	Analyzing the Audience (*APS*, Chapter 5, pp. 58–71); Using Language (*APS*, Chapter 10, pp. 130–144).
Materials/Preparation:	Different topics and roles for the audience.

Scenario

Topic: How to Prepare Breakfast.

Roles of the audience:

Role 1: First graders in the primary school.

Role 2: A group of college students.

Role 3: A group of gourmet chefs.

🕐 In-Class Procedure

PPT/Directions	活动过程描述
1. *Directions:* You are going to design a speech for your target audience regarding how to prepare breakfast. The class will be divided into several groups, each group with three members. Every member of the group will be responsible for one type of audience.	1. 教师介绍任务，所有的学生都将要设计一个演讲，话题是 How to Prepare Breakfast。全班同学将分组，每组三人。每位组员代表一类听众。因此，设计演讲时请注意，每位同学的听众都将会是不一样的。
2. Group division for the first round.	2. 分组。规则：教师要求请第一排最左边的同学数数，从1开始数，然后是2，再然后是3，数到3后再数1，这样依次数数，数1、2、3的同学分别为一个小组。

（待续）

PPT/Directions	活动过程描述
3. No. 1—Audience Type I No. 2—Audience Type II No. 3—Audience Type III	3. 教师帮助学生快速了解自己的听众：数1的同学，听众为第一类听众；数2的则为第二类；数3的为第三类。
4. Three types of audience: Type I: First graders in the primary school. Type II: A group of college students. Type III: A group of gourmet chefs.	4. 教师向全班展示这三类听众。
5. Group discussion.	5. 开始小组讨论，每个人在谈论之前有三分钟的构思时间。
6. Report, discuss and collect ideas.	6. 教师宣布小组成员相互展示自己关于自己的话题的构思与想法，时间为五分钟。其他成员可以给出修改意见（每个学生只谈论自己的想法，因为每个人的听众不一样）。
7. Reorganize the groups. All 1s form Group 2. All 2s form Group 3. All 3s form Group 1.	7. 全班重新分组。规则为：所有数1的学生为第二组，他们的听众为第二类听众；所有数2的学生为第三组，他们的听众为第三类听众；所有数3的学生为第一组，他们的听众为第一类听众。

8–10
 	
Collect and organize ideas (15–20 mins.)
• Individual contributions
• Discussion
  Select good ideas
  Organize the speech
	8. 教师告诉学生这次讨论时，全组的话题与听众都是一样的。谈论开始前，每位成员花一分钟介绍自己的构思。
	9. 然后全组进行讨论，讨论时间是八分钟。
	10. 各组形成针对各自的听众最佳演讲规划与构思。

11. Presentation time. (three mins. for each group)	11. 各组推选一位代表，向全班展示本组的成果。展示时间为每组三分钟。
12. Audience analysis.	12. 三个展示结束后，教师开始讲解听众分析。

1. The most important part of this activity is at the end when the instructor asks why different audience invoke different points. Students should easily be able to respond with the ideas that, among other things, the levels of knowledge and the needs of each audience are different.

2. In contrast to a purely demographic analysis, this activity provides a more humanistic and realistic approach to developing an accurate perception of an audience. Such a perspective will ultimately prove to be useful in developing an effective message.

Choosing Speech Topics

UNDERSTANDING TEACHING

Tell me, and I will forget. Show me, and I may remember. Involve me, and I will understand.

—*Xunzi*

In designing tasks, the instructor should take care to ensure that the task design requires active student participation and promotes the acquisition of the task's pedagogical goals.

—*Abdi Kazeroni*

TEACHER'S GUIDE (Q & A)

➤ **topic 和 title 有何不同?**

- topic 和 title 语义有时重合，有时区分。topic 一词使用更为广泛，语义外延也更广。
- 《演讲的艺术》第十版（中国版）教材区分两者（多数写作教材也区分两者）。topic 为演讲话题，title 为标题或题目。演讲准备初期需要确定的 topic 应具有语言表达和语义上的透明度，后期确定的 title 可以在语言表达上增加趣味性或神秘感。根据 *APS* 教材，演讲的第一步是"确定话题"，而最后一步是"确定标题"（参见 *APS*, p. 121）。
- 在实际操作中，topic 可以完全等同于 title，如 Unsafe Drinking Water 和 Unity and Diversity；但 Toxins on Tap 和 Be Different from Yourself 这样的表达更适合于 title，而不是严格意义上的 topic。更多的时候，选择话题时，需要从一个大的话题不断地缩小范围，一直缩小至一场演讲可以把握的范围。如从"环境"或"健康"这样的大话题，可能逐步缩小至 Unsafe Drinking Water 这样的小话题。

➤ **该教学环节何时进行?**

- 《演讲的艺术》第十版（中国版）教材中，该环节安排在第四章的"选择演讲话题（Choosing a Topic）"小节（*APS*, pp. 44–48）。学习本单元之前，学生需对第一章所涉及的公众演讲的过程及要素有基本了解，应有交流意识。
- 这是演讲准备的第一个环节——确定演讲话题。但在整个学期中，凡是遇到学生演讲选题方面出现问题的时候都有必要讲解和讨论。
- *APS* 教材的第九章中，"演讲提纲（The Preparation Outline）"小节的最后一部分

"确定演讲标题"（Give Your Speech a Title, *APS*, p. 121）与大部分学生所理解的 topic 相关，可进行区分。

- 涉及不同的演讲类型，话题选择也可能不同；同样地，话题选择也可能决定演讲的类型。相关讨论在信息性演讲和说服性演讲两章均有涉及，具体章节包括：
  A. Types of Informative Speeches: Analysis and Organization (*APS*, Chapter 13, pp. 177–184);
  B. Persuasive Speeches on Questions of Fact, Persuasive Speeches on Questions of Value, Persuasive Speeches on Questions of Policy (*APS*, Chapter 14, pp. 195–204).

➤ 该教学环节有何必要性？

- 确定话题，从某种程度上讲，是演讲成败的关键。忽视选题，可能演讲还没有开始，便已经失败了。
- 话题的选择之所以重要还在于，确定话题时，演讲者的交流目的、演讲的类型以及演讲的组织方式也将大致确定。之后的文献查阅、讲稿写作、演讲表达等环节均需与话题对应，尤其是当话题已较为具体时。

➤ 该环节的主要教学目标是什么？

- 帮助学生提高演讲准备中的选题意识，了解知识和话题的分类。
- 帮助学生拓展思路，激发思维，掌握最佳话题的特点，从话题中寻找新意。
- 帮助学生了解演讲话题、目的以及核心观点之间的逻辑关系。

➤ 最佳选题有什么标准？

从三个角度审视话题，寻找它们的交集，便可获得最佳选题：

- 本人对该话题非常熟悉，无论是已有知识体系中具备的，还是经过阅读和研究后了解的；
- 本人对该话题有激情，有强烈的表达或抒发的欲望；
- 听众对该话题有极大的兴趣。

➤ 常见的教学困难

- 学生常反映，脑子里一片空白，不知道说什么，等待教师布置话题。
- 学生即使能找到话题，也找不到有趣的切入点。
- 学生常不能有效地缩小话题范围，不能有效确定一个可以集中而深入探讨的话题。

➤ 教与学的误区

- 无论是教师还是学生，选题一节最容易被忽略。常匆忙定题，将主要精力放在选题之后的工作。岂不知，很多时候，还未开始，已注定失败。
- 知识储备不足，导致不知道该说什么。操作中，常随便选定一个话题，或者选一个容易完成的话题。
- 凭空选题，不进行必要的阅读和思考；不能有效缩小话题范围。
- 忽视选题的三个标准，只关注到一两个方面。最容易忽视的问题是：What are the audience interested in?

Goal:	To provide students with a selection of speech topics and elicit imagination and association so as to help them find out a narrow topic that they are really interested in.
Class Size:	Ideally, less than 30 students.
Time:	40 mins.
Pre-Class Reading Assignment:	Selecting a Topic and a Purpose (*APS*, Chapter 4, pp. 44–57).
Materials/Preparation:	Two lists of familiar speech topics. List 1 contains 30 broad topics and List 2 contains 30 narrower topics.

List of Topics 1

1. Building Trust Between People
2. Challenge
3. Music
4. Sports
5. Traffic Policeman
6. Friendship
7. Crimes and Laws
8. Morality
9. Building a Harmonious Society
10. Interpersonal Relations
11. Buying Private Cars
12. Measuring Happiness
13. Self-Confidence
14. Sense of Responsibility
15. Quantity and Quality
16. Age and Experience
17. Sense of Honesty
18. Job Interview
19. Optimism
20. Chance and Choice
21. Hard Work and Success
22. Expectation and Reality
23. Creative Thinking in Education

List of Topics 2

1. Mobile Phones and Global Communication
2. State Education Assistance Loans
3. Holidays and Tourism
4. Noise, a Problem Troubling People in an Intangible Way
5. On Pet-Dog Keeping
6. On the Construction of Garden-Like Cities
7. Value Our Precious Water Supply
8. Add to the Meaning of Instructor's Day
9. The Greener, the Better
10. Let Kids Enjoy Holiday
11. On the Price of Pollution
12. Stop Students from Indulging in Computer Games
13. How Far Is China Away from the Nobel Prize?
14. Smile and You'll Get a Smile in Return
15. Job Rights and Gender Equality
16. Making Drinking Water Safe
17. Golden Week Holidays
18. Honesty Is Good Business
19. Rising Prices Hurt Everyone
20. How to Lighten School Bags

24. Climate and Agriculture
25. Competition and Co-operation
26. School Rules and Regulations
27. Economic Growth and Environmental Protection
28. National Resources and Energy Saving
29. Regulating the Advertising Market
30. English Competition and My English Study

21. Importance of Reading
22. City Jams and Road Rules
23. All for One, One for All—That Is Our Motto
24. A Good Book Is a Light to the Soul
25. Books, Like Friends, Should Be Few and Well-Chosen
26. Suspicion Is the Poison of Friendship
27. Beauty Is No Use Without Brains
28. From Saving Comes Having
29. Learning Is the Enterprise of a Lifetime
30. The World Is Getting Smaller and Smaller

🕐 In-Class Procedure

PPT/Directions	活动过程描述
Pre-Class Assignment	**课前任务**
2–3 *Directions:* Each group will receive a list of topics which contains 30 broad speech topics. You should find your own topic, the sequence number of which matches your student ID. Think about the topic: What does it mean? How would you define it? From what perspective will you view it? And next time, we should expect to hear everybody's definition of his or her topic. You may also see the attached file of the list of topics sent to your public mailbox.	1. 将学生分为小组，一组五人左右。 2. 课前任务：为节约课堂时间，并给学生更多的准备和思考时间，在前一次课结束之前，便将材料中List of Topics 1（参见Materials/Preparation）发给每一个小组。课后，将电子稿发到学生的公共邮箱或分享到课程平台，以便学生查看。 3. 学生按照自己的学号（假定学号从一号到30号），每人领取一道题目，课后思考对题目的理解，并准备下次课上汇报。鼓励学生用自己的语言表达自己的想法，可参考字典定义，但不直接使用字典措词。每位学生的题目不同，鼓励学生同时关注其他题目。
In-Class Procedure	**课堂活动描述**
4–5 My topic: ＿＿＿＿＿＿＿ My definition of the topic: ＿＿＿＿＿＿ A narrow topic I'm interested in: ＿＿＿＿	4. 小组讨论三分钟，每人陈述对自己话题的理解。小组讨论时，应养成有一位组员记笔记的习惯。 5. 给每个小组分发材料List of Topics 2（参见Materials/Preparation）。每人在这30个选项中寻找与自己原来的话题最相关的一项，并向其他组员陈述理由。如果学生感觉这份话题单中没有合适的，可以自己缩小话题范围。 （五分钟内。）

（待续）

PPT/Directions	活动过程描述
	6. 下一环节为小组陈述与教师指导环节。该环节要求以小组为单位，所有成员到讲台前进行陈述，陈述线索如幻灯片4–5所示。每人的陈述时间不得超过40秒钟，应给出简单解释。
	7. 事先准备好两个电子文档，即两个Lists of Topics，最好是左右并排的两个窗口，学生陈述时可选中相关话题，以便听众理解。

8.
 	
My topic:
  17. Sense of Honesty
A narrow topic I'm interested in:
  18. Honesty Is Good Business
	8. 这一环节中教师的指导作用至关重要。若学生的陈述中肯，应予以鼓励；若学生的理解或视野狭窄，则教师应予以启发。教师的启发将是学生最感兴趣的部分。例如，有同学认为与自己选择的第17项话题相关的小话题为List 2中的第18项Honesty Is Good Business。

9. Building Trust Between People ↕ Honesty Is Good Business ↕ ? Sense of Honesty	9. 这时，教师可以适当引导：Building Trust Between People 与 Honesty Is Good Business 之间的联系更为紧密。 10. 教师的引导以尊重学生的兴趣与知识体系为基础，拓展思维为主要目的，而并非给学生提供一个"正确"答案。当然，允许学生从My topic 一项开始即选择所提供的话题单之外感兴趣的话题。 （以30人的班级来看，整个陈述与讨论环节需要约30分钟。教师点评为鼓励性的、选择性的，不一定给每位学生提供反馈，以避免重复、单调。）
After-Class Assignment (Extension)	**以下为活动的拓展部分，可供选择使用。**
11. My topic: (Please provide both the sequence number and the topic in List 1) _____ My definition of the topic: _____ A narrow topic I'm interested in: (Please provide both the sequence number and the topic in List 2. You may also provide a topic you've narrowed by yourself.) _____ My reason(s): _____	11. 要求每一位学生按照左侧幻灯片所示的线索对自己的演讲选题进行书面陈述。陈述格式如幻灯片11所示。当然，允许学生从My topic 一项开始就选择List of Topics 之外自己喜欢的话题。 12. 书面作业（最好是电子文本）由小组汇总，最后汇总到课代表处。要求课后第二天内完成。（如已使用网络教学平台，则第12-15步骤均设置为学生个人上传。其他程序，教师可以在网络平台上进行相应设置。）

（待续）

PPT/Directions	活动过程描述
13. Five topics I like best: (Provide the sequence number in List 1 only.) _____ Five topics I like least: (Provide the sequence number in List 1 only.) _____	13. 学习委员将所有书面陈述汇总到一个Word文档中，并将文档发至班级电子邮箱，同时发送一份调查表（如左侧幻灯片13所示），需要每位同学填写。这也意味着，每个人需要浏览所有同学的书面陈述。调查表需于两天之内反馈给学习委员。 14. 学习委员汇总统计，并将统计结果反馈给教师。 15. 教师将统计结果在下一次课时反馈给学生。同时，务必给最不受欢迎的五个题目提供解决方案。
(Prepare for Term Project)	**（准备学期演讲项目）**
16–17 Prepare for your term project.	16. 学生经过思考、讨论、再反思之后，确定自己最喜欢、同时听众也喜欢的话题。话题可在教师那边备案。以此话题为起点，准备学期演讲项目，并在随后各章节的学习过程中完成和不断充实自己的演讲稿。 17. 允许学生在学习过程中更换更喜爱的话题。

Comments/Reflections

1. Most instructors will find this activity recommendable for its multifold functions. Firstly, it provides beginning English public speakers with a pool of topics, who often feel that they don't know what to say. Students don't have to stick to the topic assigned to them, but the assigned topic can serve as a starting point for exploration. Second, students learn to dig deep into a broad topic and then narrow it, which is even more important. Third, the activity would be of great attraction to instructors who require a term speech project of students toward the end of the semester. The activity is a good starting point for a term project.

2. This is a typical small-class activity in which everybody speaks to the class. However, instructors of a large class may also find it helpful to provide students with resources of topics, and hopefully, help students find an interesting topic to prepare early for the big speech day at the end of the semester. The more time is allowed for preparation, the more students will learn and the better performance they will give. The only difference made to the original procedure would be that not everybody has to speak in public.

3. The topics in the two lists can be adapted.

（供稿人：黄珊 华东交通大学；改编人：田朝霞）

Goal:	To stimulate students' creativity in construing the topics from the "FLTRP Cup" (formerly known as "CCTV Cup") English Public Speaking Contest.
Class Size:	Any.
Time:	10–15 mins.
Pre-Class Reading Assignment:	Speaking in Competitions (*APS*, Chapter 16, pp. 234–252).
Materials/Preparation:	A. Three lists of topics from the "FLTRP Cup" English Public Speaking Contest.

Topics from the "FLTRP Cup" (2002–2005)

2002	My Virtual University
2003	The Future Is Now
2004	Man and the Internet
2005	The Greatest Invention in My Eyes

Topics from the "FLTRP Cup" (2006–2010)

2006	Unity and Diversity
2007	Global Citizen Begins at Home
2008	1+1=2?
2009	Culture Smart or Science Intelligent?
2010	_____ Is My Top Concern

Topics from the "FLTRP Cup" (2011–2014)

2011	A Word That Has Changed the World
2012	What We Cannot Afford to Lose
2013	When Socrates Meets Confucius
2014	Change the Unchangeable

B.   Examples of the subtitles given by prize winners.

A Word That Has Changed the World
—Concentration
—Contradiction
—Laziness
—Listen
—SHE
—We
—Wisdom in Children
—Wow
—Smile

What We Cannot Afford to Lose
—Independent Judgment
—Pioneering Spirit
—Dialect
—Acknowledging Our Ignorance
—Don't Lose Your Apple
—Innocence
—Stand on the Edge of Courage
—Mercy
—Hope

In-Class Procedure

PPT/Directions	活动过程描述
2. *Directions:* You've received a list of topics from the "FLTRP Cup" English Public Speaking Contest. Discuss with your group members for about five minutes: How do you interpret the topic? How do you define your central idea? Can you provide a subtitle?	1. 将事先准备好的三份"外研社杯"全国英语演讲大赛定题演讲题目单（准备多份复印件）分发给各小组，每个小组领取一份即可。 2. 小组讨论：你如何解读题目？你会从哪些方面展开？你的核心观点是什么？是否能给出一个副标题？（五分钟。）
3–4 Guided Class Discussion Group Discussion	3. 小组讨论完毕，提问几名学生，学生仅进行简短汇报，不必展开。提问时，应同时在PPT上呈现相应的题目（参见 Materials/Preparation A）。（1–2分钟。） 4. 将 Materials B 部分获奖选手对 A Word That Has Changed the World 和 What We Cannot Afford to Lose 两个题目给出的副标题呈现于PPT上，请学生进行小组讨论和评价。（3–5分钟内完成。）
5. 历年《"外研社杯"全国英语演讲大赛》 《英语演讲选评100篇》（2002–2005） 《英语演讲选评100篇》（2006–2010） speaking.unipus.cn ustage. unipus. cn	5. 鼓励学生课后查询相关资料，了解获奖选手对大赛题目的精彩解读。

1. This is a mini-activity, the main purpose of which is to broaden students' horizon and stimulate thinking and creativity. The most valuable part is to present to students the prize winners' insightful construal of the topics.

2. In an even briefer version, the instructor may skip over Step 2, and directly invite impromptu comments from students, and then present the examples.

3. It's not necessary to analyze each topic unless students are to participate in a contest. Several good examples are enough to arouse students' curiosity, and hopefully they will find out more after class by themselves.

4. Meanwhile, it is important to see a difference between speaking competitions and English Public Speaking (EPS) class. It is important to build every student's self-esteem in EPS. Teaching would be a failure if average students feel that they are irrelevant when this activity is being conducted.

10.3

Choosing Topics for Speeches: A Breath of Fresh Air

Goal: To provide students with the opportunity to explore new areas of interest while developing imaginative speech topics.

Class Size: Any.

Time: 30 mins.

Pre-Class Reading Assignment: None; or Selecting a Topic and a Purpose (*APS*, Chapter 4, pp. 44–57); Creativity (*APS*, Chapter 16, pp. 236–237).

Materials/Preparation: Questions which help students explore extensively about the topic.

Questions About Earth/Water/Air/Fire

1. What is your own personal concept of this element? What ideas come to your mind when you say the word?
2. What did your family teach you about this element? Do they respect it? Do they abuse it? How?
3. What will you teach your children about this element?
4. Who or what lives in this element? How does this affect our lives?
5. What are some of the natural occurrences brought on by this element? How do they affect us? How do we affect them?
6. What are the symbols of this element? What do they mean in our time?
7. What did this element mean to ancient people? How did they use it?
8. What has this element meant to religion? In ancient times? How have people worshipped it?
9. What are some of the stories or legends about how man came to use this element? What lessons did people learn about it in the legends? How do we apply or interpret those lessons today?
10. Who or what are the enemies of this element? Friends?
11. How does this element add to our lives? How does it take away?
12. How do we protect this element? How do we endanger it?
13. How have we harnessed this element? What does it add to our lives? Do we use it for healing? Recreation? Survival? How?
14. What requires this element for survival? What would happen without it?
15. Does this element remind you of certain literary works? What are they about?

PPT/Directions	活动过程描述
2. *Directions:* Now each group has been assigned a broad topic—Earth, Water, Air, or Fire, and has received a list of 15 questions. You will discuss about the questions and try to generate a list of 10 possible speech topics from your answers. Remember that the topics are not limited to environmental issues. Try to examine any aspect of life affected by the element you are discussing about. You will have 20 minutes to complete this task.	1. 四个话题——Earth、Water、Air及Fire，各小组领取或分配其中一个。给大家一分钟时间，讨论这样的演讲话题可以从哪些方面展开？ 2. 将事先准备好的问题单（参见 Materials/Preparation）发给每个小组。学生要针对所分配的话题对所列的每个问题进行回答，讨论目的是寻找有趣的演讲题目。每个小组需要提供至少10个有新意的题目。小组讨论时间为20分钟。 3. 教师旁听、观察或参与各小组讨论，必要时给予提示，但不要介入太多。问题单上的许多题目，学生可能并不熟悉。可让学生跳过这些题目，因为讨论的目的是找好的选题，而不是问题本身。 4. 讨论完毕，请各小组代表向大家汇报讨论结果，并请全班判断这些演讲题目是否有趣。一般情况下，各小组都能收获之前未曾想到的好题目。
After-Class Assignment (Extension)	**拓展活动**
5. 	5. 讨论过程中会遇到暂时无法回答的问题，鼓励学生课后查阅图书馆或网上文献，鼓励学生查阅索引（Index）。应扩大搜索范围，不仅查阅"环境"与"科学"主题，还应扩展至"人文"、"艺术"、"心理学"等。也可以考虑给不同的小组分配不同的学科分类，进行资料查阅。 6. 这些文献查阅工作学生是否做了？做的结果如何？这些都需要检查。建议两种方法： A. 要求每位学生（或小组）一周后再次提交一个演讲题目，并说明为什么选择该题目？ B. 如果该课程要求学生完成一项大的学期演讲任务，那么这个题目也可作为学期演讲题目。后续工作将随课程展开而跟进。

Comments/Reflections

1. We often observe that, students' real problem lies in at least two aspects: limited knowledge and poor thinking skills (e.g., following the herd or thinking inside confined to the box). This activity addresses precisely the problem. The listed questions encourage students to think outside the box by extensively associating a broad topic with various subjects.

2. The questions may also stimulate students to do research after class, arousing their information awareness and hence enhancing their information literacy (see Unit 11).

3. The instructor may well give a list of different broad topics and adapt the questions to specific purposes. For example, students may be required to explore topics like "North, South, East and West—Exploring the World Around Us."

4. For instructors who give students' term speech assignment, this activity is especially a good starting point.

本活动的设计基于以下文献来源：Woodside, Daria. (1995). Choosing Topics for Speeches: A Breath of Fresh Air. In Lucas, Stephen E. (ed.) *Selections from the Speech Communication Teacher, 1991–1994*. Madison, Wisconsin: McGraw-Hill. 14–15.

Information Literacy

UNDERSTANDING TEACHING

I never teach my pupils; I only attempt to provide the conditions in which they can learn.

—*Albert Einstein*

When you wish to instruct, be brief; that men's minds take in quickly what you say, learn its lesson, and retain it faithfully. Every word that is unnecessary only pours over the side of a brimming mind.

—*Cicero*

TEACHER'S GUIDE (Q & A)

➤ **什么是"信息素养（information literacy）"？**

- 信息素养通常指搜寻、提取、分析甄别、选择以及使用信息的能力。
- 信息素养过去主要与图书馆的使用能力相联系，是任何学术研究不可或缺的部分；而现在已扩展为使用各种信息渠道的能力，并成为全球信息化时代需要人们具备的基本能力，更是大学生的基本素质之一。
- 从更广泛的意义上讲，信息素养至少包括信息意识、信息知识、信息能力和信息道德四个方面。

➤ **该教学环节何时进行？**

- 信息素养这部分在美国高校的教学中，是公众演讲（Public Speaking: Introduction to Speech Composition）的一项重要内容，而中国学生大多数没有这方面的系统训练。
- 信息获取能力的培养贯穿演讲准备的各个环节，凡需要信息支撑之处，便需要这种能力。
- 《演讲的艺术》第十版（中国版）教材中，信息素养虽未单独成章，但有关信息知识与能力的内容贯穿于多个环节，至少包括：
  A. Choosing a Topic (*APS*, Chapter 4, pp. 45–48);
  B. Statistics, Testimony (*APS*, Chapter 6, pp. 76–83);
  C. Using Evidence (*APS*, Chapter 14, pp. 208–209).

- 信息道德也是信息素养的重要组成部分，集中在第二章有关抄袭的小节：Plagiarism (*APS*, Chapter 2, pp. 26–30)。

➤ 该教学环节有何必要性？

- 中国学生的信息意识较为薄弱，主要表现为，写作时很少查阅资料，多为个人感想的抒发，抑或人云亦云。其演讲给人的感觉是空洞、乏味。因此提高学生的信息意识与能力极为必要和紧迫。
- 信息素养直接关系到演讲是否有理有据，也直接关系到能否产出高质量的演讲稿。
- 信息素养对于信息性演讲更是必不可少。信息性演讲的基本标准之一——准确性（accuracy），主要依靠信息来源支撑。

➤ 该环节的主要教学目标和内容是什么？

- 培养和提高学生的信息意识，学会判断何时何地需要信息的支撑。
- 帮助学生提高逻辑严谨的思维习惯，最终达到演讲内容充实、有理有据的教学目标。
- 帮助学生了解和掌握搜寻、提取、分析甄别、选择以及使用信息的方法。
  - A. 如何查阅学校图书馆的图书文献？
  - B. 如何使用教育网络提供的数字信息平台？
  - C. 互联网上有哪些常用的搜索引擎？
  - D. 如何判断信息资源（特别是网上资源）的可信度与价值？
  - E. 同类信息中如何选择最佳信息？
  - F. 如何鉴别演讲中信息的质量？

➤ 常见的教学困难

- 学生的信息意识较为薄弱，常不能意识到提供支撑信息的必要性和重要性。
- 查阅信息需要花费大量时间和精力，学生有时不配合，敷衍了事。
- 查阅资料主要在课后完成，教师很难检查学生任务完成的真实情况。
- 学生在使用信息时，常出现各种抄袭情况而自己并未意识到；有时甚至学习各种抄袭方法。

➤ 常见的教学误区

- 如果有人说"抽烟有害"，难道我应该质疑吗？（无论如何作答，均需要提供依据，而不是人云亦云。）
- 演讲主要是抒发感想，感动别人，几乎不需要查阅资料。信息的使用对演讲的意义不大。
- 很多的观点或主张，不需要提供支撑信息，因为这些观点是"显而易见"的。
- 太多信息的使用，尤其是数据的摄入似乎与演讲的语言风格不相称。可能使得演讲的内容枯燥，并带有学术论文的气氛，以致不能感染听众。

Why Should You Believe What Others Say? # 11.1

Goal:	To arouse students' awareness of the importance of reliable information as evidence and help students develop critical thinking ability.
Class Size:	Any.
Time:	20 mins.
Pre-Class Reading Assignment:	Statistics, Testimony (*APS*, Chapter 6, pp. 76–83).
Materials/Preparation:	A topic card.

Topic Card

1. Tell your classmates how dangerous online shopping is.
2. Tell your classmates how harmful smoking is to one's health.

🕐 In-Class Procedure

PPT/Directions	活动过程描述
1–2 *Directions:* Choose one topic. ↓ Prepare for three minutes. ↓ Speak for up to two minutes.	1. 在幻灯片上展示出两个演讲话题（参见 Materials/Preparation）。 2. 让学生自愿选择其中一个话题，准备三分钟。并告知，之后会邀请两位学生进行不超过两分钟的演讲。鼓励学生展示精彩的即兴演讲。

4.
 	
Notes
• Sub-point 1?
  ??
• Sub-point 2?
  ??
• Sub-point 3?
  ??
	3. 先后邀请选择了不同话题的两位学生进行两分钟的即兴演讲。
	4. 演讲之前，要求听众做简要笔记，重点记录演讲人的观点以及所提供的论据。可参照左侧幻灯片所示的笔记框架。
	5. 两名学生演讲完毕。教师邀请其他学生简单复述两人的观点和所陈述的理由，一方面检查学生听力理解情况，另一方面梳理清楚演讲人的内容线索。

（待续）

PPT/Directions	活动过程描述
6–7 Is online shopping really dangerous? Is smoking harmful to one's health? • Did the speaker provide reasons? • Are the reasons claims or facts? • Can the reasons justify the claim? • How do you know they are facts? • Why should you believe it? …	6. 小组讨论五分钟，每个小组仅负责一个话题。讨论的主要议题是：我是否相信他（她）说的？为什么？ 7. 邀请小组代表陈述讨论结果。教师应有意识地引导学生关注观点与事实的区别，唤醒学生的信息意识。特别注意提醒学生，诸如"许多科学家都证明了……""大家都知道……"这样的陈述不具备说服力。培养学生养成独立思考和思辨的习惯。
8–9 Supporting Details • Statistics Sources? • Testimony Expert testimony (sources?) Peer testimony (sources?)	8. 引入或复习：什么样的理由是可信的？ 9. 鼓励学生课后查找支撑（或反驳）两个观点的理由。可指定两位同学在下一次上课时向全班汇报。特别强调支撑信息的可靠来源。

Comments/Reflections

1. A big problem of Chinese students is that many of them simply don't consciously seek for grounds for suspicion or doubt. When they hear people repeat that online shopping is bad or smoking is bad, many just take it. And when the noise is loud they would even feel ashamed or unsafe if they are not in the crowd. So when "everybody knows" something it would definitely be taken as a fact.

2. This activity is to arouse students' awareness of questioning in the first place. Even though "everybody knows," we still need to ask, "Why does everybody think so?" "But is it true even though everybody thinks so?" "Why should we believe it simply because everybody does?" "What kind of facts can support the claim?" An interesting logical fallacy is that if what everybody believes is really true, there won't be such an issue. Besides, students need to learn to identify, evaluate and weigh opposing ideas and facts.

3. Do whatever is appropriate to help students make independent judgment.

Goal: To help students understand information literacy through "learning by doing and teaching."

Class Size: 40 students.

Time: Less than 25 mins, not including pre-class assignments.

Pre-Class Reading Assignment: Statistics, Testimony (*APS*, Chapter 6, pp. 76–83).

Materials/Preparation:
A. Video clip: "Yoga: Uniting Mind, Body, and Spirit" (*APS*, Video 13.3).
B. What is information literacy?

What Is Information Literacy?

The well-established definition of information literacy is outlined in the Final Report of the American Library Association (ALA) Presidential Committee on Information Literacy: "To be information literate, a person must be able to recognize when information is needed and have the ability to locate, evaluate, and use effectively the needed information" (ALA, 1989: 1).

C. Use of expert testimony in "Yoga: Uniting Mind, Body, and Spirit."

Use of Expert Testimony in "Yoga: Uniting Mind, Body, and Spirit"

1. **As Stella Weller says in her book,** *Yoga: Finding Balance and Serenity in Everyday Life*, yoga is the practice of uniting one's mind, body, and spirit.

2. **As Vimla Lalvani, author of** *The Power of Yoga*, **writes:** "Correct breathing rejuvenates the entire system by sending increased oxygen into the bloodstream to nourish and revitalize the internal organs... The deeper you breathe, the calmer the mind becomes."

3. **Donna Farhi, author of five books on yoga, emphasized** that yoga affects the whole body and the whole person. "Each movement," she says, "demands that we hone some aspect of our consciousness and use ourselves in a whole new way."

D. Prompts for discussion: What kind of information is needed?

What Kind of Information Is Needed If I Make a Speech to My Classmates?

- Speaker analysis: Who am I? Why should people listen to me?
- Audience analysis: Who is the audience? Why should they be interested?
- Purpose analysis: Why do I give this speech?
- Content analysis: What kind of information is important?
- Research methods: Where to find the information? How to evaluate it?

In-Class Procedure

PPT/Directions	活动过程描述
Pre-Class Assignments	**课前任务**
1–2 Assignments: A. Find out on the Internet about the definitions of "information literacy." Evaluate the information obtained from multiple sources. B. Watch the video clip, "Yoga: Uniting Mind, Body, and Spirit," which you can find in the CD-ROM accompanying *APS*. Locate where sources of information are given. Analyze the function of those sources. C. Watch the video clip, "Yoga: Uniting Mind, Body, and Spirit." Suppose you are going to make a speech under the same title to your classmates. Discuss how your speech might be different from the video, what preparations you need to make, and how you are going to complete the preparations.	1. 在前一节课结束之前，询问学生是否听说过"信息素养"这一术语。告诉学生这已成为当代大学生必备的基本素质，激发学生进一步了解的兴趣。 2. 将三项任务分配给不同的小组，每个小组承担一项任务。要求小组在下一次课时进行三分钟的小组汇报，并制作PPT。 A. 到网上查找"信息素养"的定义，需要提供多处来源，鉴别来源的权威性，并给出理由。 B. 观看"Yoga: Uniting Mind, Body, and Spirit"的演讲视频（参见Materials/Preparation A），找出演讲者引用专家观点的部分，并讨论其作用。 C. 观看"Yoga: Uniting Mind, Body, and Spirit"的演讲视频，并讨论：如果你们要进行一场相同题目的演讲，需要做哪些准备？如何实施这些准备？ 提醒学生： A. 汇报方式应模拟教师授课时的微型讲座。 B. 强调：小组汇报的质量将以听众听讲的效果作为标准。听众是否听懂了？是否赞同？

（待续）

PPT/Directions	活动过程描述
In-Class Procedure	**课堂活动描述**
3–4 Research into information literacy: • Enough sources? • Authoritativeness? Why?	3. 邀请一组学生（可派代表，也可小组合作）进行有关信息素养定义的搜索与查找的微型讲座。 4. 微型讲座完毕后，演讲人邀请听众对疑难处进行提问。教师充当听众，从学生角度，进行提问。关注两个方面：一、是否提供了多个信息来源？信息量是否充足？最好能有10项左右；二、学生对信息的评价是否合理？ （五分钟。）
5. Examples of expert testimony: • As Stella Weller says in her book, *Yoga: Finding Balance and Serenity in Everyday Life…* • As Vimla Lalvani, author of *The Power of Yoga*, writes… • Donna Farhi, author of five books on yoga, emphasized…	5. 邀请准备第二项任务的小组进行微型讲座。 6. 演讲人邀请听众对疑难处进行提问。教师充当学生，从学生角度，进行提问。重点考察两个方面：是否对演讲中的专家观点进行了准确定位？是否对专家观点的作用进行了合理评估？ （五分钟。）
7. What kind of information is needed if I make the speech to my classmates?	7. 邀请准备第三项任务的小组之一充当小老师，进行微型讲座。讲座完毕，请其他准备相同任务的小组进行简短补充，然后请听众提问，并解答。 （六分钟。）
8. What kind of information is needed? • Speaker analysis • Audience analysis • Purpose analysis • Content analysis • Research method (See Materials/Preparation D.)	8. 教师重新回到自己的教师角色，组织全班讨论，引导学生思考在准备材料时需考虑的方面（如左侧幻灯片所示）。 　A. 提醒学生真实的演讲环境：学生（演讲者和听众）可能并没有瑜伽经历，在这种情况下如何进行好一场介绍瑜伽精神的演讲呢？ 　B. 引导学生重点讨论搜索相关信息的途径和方法，包括图书馆和互联网。 （五分钟。）
	9. 指定一位学生课后重新完成第三项任务，下次课上将充当小老师，进行一场三分钟的微型讲座，对Materials/Preparation D 中的问题逐一回应。 （一分钟。）

1. This activity provides students with an opportunity to get acquainted with information literacy—its definition, importance and enhancement. This is of vital significance to students who are not used to providing concrete reliable evidence for their point of view.

2. The speech, "Yoga: Uniting Mind, Body, and Spirit," is good enough for a variety of activities in class. In this activity, it is a very good example to show how the speaker's information literacy helps her establish credibility. In fact, it is in the whole process of research prior to the speech writing that information literacy is justifiably improved.

3. Besides the video clip, "Yoga: Uniting Mind, Body, and Spirit," there are more good examples. Two video clips, "Secure Yourself Online" and "The Hidden World of Chili Peppers," present how effective use of expert testimony enhances the impact of speech. Both provide a version in need of improvement and an improved version. These examples, which are found in the DVD accompanying *APS Teacher's Manual*, are highly recommended.

4. An important teaching strategy here is to give students full emotional support and help them confidently perform the role of an instructor. While teaching, students will acquire full understanding of the content. Or, whatever confusion that may arise will stimulate them to explore afterwards.

（供稿人：陈志红 华中师范大学；改编人：田朝霞）

So What If You Found It on the Internet: An Exercise in Evaluating Web-Based Information?

11.3

Goal: To teach students how to evaluate information obtained from Web sites for validity and reliability and develop their critical thinking and evaluative skills of Internet sources.

Class Size: 40 students.

Time: 20 mins, not including pre-class assignments.

Pre-Class Reading Assignment: Statistics, Testimony (*APS*, Chapter 6, pp. 76–83).

Materials/Preparation: A. A checklist for Internet sources.

A Checklist for Internet Sources

- What is the site's purpose? Can its information be biased?

- Who sponsors the site? What are the organization's values or goals? Can you contact the sponsors?

- Is the information in the site well-documented? Does it provide citations to sources used in obtaining the information? Are individual articles signed or attributed?

- When was it published? Is the date of the last revision posted somewhere on the page?

- What are the author's credentials? Is the author cited frequently in other sources?

- How was the value of the Web-based information you've found compared with other available sources, such as printed?

B. Topics for research.

Topics for Research

1. What are the causes of obesity?
2. What are the causes of psychological depression among college students?
3. Is global warming a fact or a fantasy?
4. Is the steel industry a falling industry?

⏱ In-Class Procedure

PPT/Directions	活动过程描述
Pre-Class Assignments	**课前任务**

2.
 	
Guidelines for Presentation
 	
Source 1 (the most reliable and valid)
· Opinion
· Source
· Evaluation
(See the checklist.)
Source 2
…
Source 5 (the least reliable and valid)
…
	1. 将几个研究问题（参见 Materials/Preparation B）分配给学生，一个小组只需承担一个问题。
	
	2. 告诉学生本次作业的主要任务不是确定一个合理答案。要求学生：
	
	  A. 在网络上搜寻相关信息——研究、评论、介绍等。查询的来源不得少于15项。然后对这些信息进行评估，需要参照 Materials/Preparation A（发给学生复印件，或将评估表电子文档放在网络平台）。
	
	  B. 挑选其中有代表性的五项进行重点分析。下次课上需进行四分钟的口头陈述。提醒学生陈述时不必逐条回答，应进行必要的整合。

In-Class Procedure	**课堂活动描述**
3. What are the five most important standards for Internet sources?	3. 给各小组两分钟准备时间，整理笔记，准备上台汇报。 4. 邀请各三组代表上台，汇报网上信息查找与评估的结果。 5. 在每一组陈述后，邀请其他小组的学生补充、提问或质疑。 6. 之后，小组讨论三分钟，按照重要性递减的顺序，列出评估网上信息可靠性的五个标准。 7. 各小组汇报所总结的标准，教师引导学生对比结果，筛选重要而简便的评估标准。

Comments/Reflections

1. As almost every student is now exposed to enormously rich sources of information about every topic imaginable, it is really necessary to evaluate the Internet sources. This activity is designed for this purpose.

2. Given that this activity does not examine students' own understanding of the given topics, the instructor should make sure that students do not focus on finding a good answer to the questions. They are expected to find different opinions concerning the topics and try to evaluate the information based on the checklist.

3. Make sure that the group work is effectively done. It may be necessary to assign a specific role to everybody. The group may also need to meet for discussion or group discussion online.

4. Encourage students to make use of the checklist whenever the Internet sources are needed.

本活动的设计基于以下文献来源: Hanson, Trudy L. (2004). So What If You Found It on the Internet: An Exercise in Evaluating Web-Based Information. In Lucas, Stephen E. (ed.) *Selections from the Speech Communication Teacher, 1999–2002*. Madison, Wisconsin: McGraw-Hill. 67.

Critical Thinking

UNDERSTANDING TEACHING

The most important step in developing skillful speech is to think before speaking.

—*Allan Lokos*

Not everything that counts can be counted and not everything that can be counted counts.

—*William Bruce Cameron*

He who asks a question is a fool for five minutes; he who does not ask a question remains a fool forever.

—*Chinese proverb*

TEACHER'S GUIDE (Q & A)

➤ **什么是"思辨（critical thinking）"？**

- critical thinking 的翻译版本众多，包括"思辨"、"批判性思维"、"审辨性思维"等，这些译法均受到不同程度的质疑。我们这里不探究其翻译措词本身，仅关注其在演讲中的基本含义。简而言之，思辨要求演讲做到至少三点：第一，逻辑清晰、严密；第二，有理有据，理据充分；第三，有独立的、开放的视角与观点。思辨强调演讲的内容本身及其内在逻辑。

➤ **该教学环节何时进行？**

- 在《演讲的艺术》第十版（中国版）的第一章，卢卡斯教授专门讨论了公众演讲与思辨的关系（APS, pp. 7-8）。可以说，思辨与演讲形影不离，只要有观点的地方，便有思辨的要求。
- 除了纵向渗透于演讲的整个过程，横向渗透于各演讲类型以外，APS教材中集中探讨思辨的章节还包括：
  A. Supporting Your Ideas (APS, Chapter 6, pp. 72–87);
  B. Connectives (APS, Chapter 7, pp. 97–100);
  C. Types of Informative Speeches: Analysis and Organization (APS, Chapter 13, pp. 177–184);

D. Persuasive Speeches on Questions of Fact, Persuasive Speeches on Questions of Value, Persuasive Speeches on Questions of Policy (*APS*, Chapter 14, pp. 195–204);

E. Using Evidence (*APS*, Chapter 14, pp. 208–209).

其中"连接词〔Connectives〕"小节为语篇逻辑的语言体现形式。

- 该教学环节可以穿插在以上任何环节，或在评价学生演讲稿的过程中进行。

➤ **该教学环节有何必要性？**

- 思辨关注观点之间的逻辑关联、证据本身的可信度以及事实与观点之间的差别，是演讲内容方面成败的关键。无论是什么类型的演讲，均要求思辨能力。
- 中国学生常被认为思辨能力薄弱，这不仅包括思维习惯方面的问题，也存在知识储备方面的问题。思辨训练在中国高校更具有现实意义。

➤ **该环节的主要教学目标是什么？**

- 提高学生对观点之间逻辑关系的辨别能力。
- 提高学生辨别、组织以及评估论点的能力。
- 提高学生对推理中的各种逻辑谬误的辨别能力（可参见 Unit 19）。
- 培养学生系统地解决问题的能力，避免从不同侧面阐述时在价值观原则上的不一致。
- 提高学生辨别观点以及其他各种信息的相关性与重要性。
- 培养学生独立思考的习惯。

➤ **常见的教学困难**

- 思辨能力要求学生时刻关注全局与细节的关系、论点与论据的关系。这一要求不仅依赖于良好的思维习惯本身，还依赖于学生的知识储备，因此是一项长期的教学目标。
- 思辨能力要求学生学会对论据不充分的论点进行质疑。许多中国学生习惯于接受别人的观点，尤其是伪装之下的权威观点。要培养思辨能力，必须帮助学生培养善于质疑的思维习惯。
- 学生因各种原因，做不到花足够的时间进行广泛阅读与认真研究，而这两点都是思辨能力培养的必要条件。
- 部分学生片面地追求新意，而常忽视整体逻辑。

➤ **教与学的误区**

- 思辨就是"反驳"，就是"批判"。
- 思辨就是观点越新越好，演讲比赛要想获胜，首先要有一鸣惊人的观点。
- 思辨主要是思维方法训练，与知识积累关系不大。

Goal: To help students understand the distinction between facts and opinions and encourage them to consciously support their points with hard facts.

Class Size: Any.

Time: 20–25 mins.

Pre-Class Reading Assignment: None.

Materials/Preparation: A. A list of statements.

Fact or Opinion?

1. My father makes the most delicious spaghetti dinners in the world.
2. I ate three meatballs with my spaghetti dinner.
3. My mother made salad to eat with our spaghetti dinner.
4. Dad uses Grandma's secret recipe to make spaghetti sauce.
5. Audrey Hepburn was a great actress.
6. Lu Xun won the Nobel Prize in Literature.
7. The population of the United States increases each year.
8. Beijing provides more job opportunities for young people.
9. Dancing is fun.
10. Audrey Hepburn is beautiful.
11. Business majors make more money than education majors five years after graduation.
12. Everyone should go to college.

Key:

1. O	2. F	3. F	4. F	5. O	6. ? (Factual Error)
7. F	8. O	9. O	10. O	11. ?	12. O

B. A piece of speech writing (no more than 500 words) from a student. (Copies may be needed for group discussion.)

PPT/Directions	活动过程描述

1.
 	
Two Phases of the Activity
 	
• Exercise: Fact or opinion?
  Fact v. Opinion
• Discussion: Speech analysis
  More facts or more opinions?
• (Discussion: Critical thinking
  Facts always facts?)
	1. 活动概述：本活动主要引导学生区分"事实"与"观点"。有些学生还没有细想过它们的区别；有些学生做还没有意识到它们有时并不像想象中那样容易区分。本活动分三个阶段：
	
	A. 让学生做练习题，并自己总结事实与观点之间的区别。
	
	B. 让学生分析一篇讲稿，了解"事实"的使用率。
	
	C.（拓展阶段，可选择不做）引导学生讨论两者之间的辩证关系，培养敏锐、严密的思辨能力。

2. **Phase 1** *Directions:* A point often needs evidence to support. The most powerful evidence is often based on hard facts. Hence facts speak louder than words. However, it is not as easy to distinguish between facts and opinions as is often thought. Here is a list of statements. Decide whether they are facts or opinions, and then try to find out the major difference between facts and opinions.	2. 活动第一阶段。让学生判断 Material/Preparation A 中句子是事实还是观点。这些陈述应逐个在幻灯片上呈现，学生逐句判断。 当遇到不同见解时，可保留不同见解，此时不必深究正确答案，如第 11 句。 第 6 句为事实错误。若学生判断为 fact，则应指出。 （五分钟。）

3.
 	
Fact or Opinion?
 	
• Fact
  Objective
  What happened or exists
• Opinion
  Subjective; belief
	3. 让学生讨论事实与观点之间的区别。可以采用教师组织全班讨论的方式，也可采用先进行小组讨论，再进行班级汇报的形式。
	
	教师将学生的讨论结果展示于屏幕上，如左侧幻灯片所示。

4. **Phase 2** **Are there facts at all?**	4. 第二阶段。教师将事先准备好的一份学生演讲稿分发到各组。将讲稿分为几个部分，分配给各小组。各小组需要找出自己负责的部分总共有多少陈述句，多少句观点，多少句事实。 讲稿选择应具代表性。一般情况下，学生会感叹"事实"真是太少了。 提醒学生在讲稿准备过程中应尽量多地展现事实。

（待续）

PPT/Directions	活动过程描述
Extended Procedure	**拓展活动**
5. (Phase 3) A. Fact or Opinion? • Lu Xun won the Nobel Prize in Literature. • Business majors make more money than education majors five years after graduation. B. Now They Are Facts! • Lu Xun has been described by Nobel Laureate Kenzaburō Ōe as "the greatest writer Asia produced in the 20th century." • A survey (Roach, 2006) shows that 95% of business majors at ABC make more money than average education majors five years after graduation.	5. 这部分为拓展活动（第三阶段），只有当学生对前两部分掌握情况较好时选择使用。（切记：学生如果还没有弄清事实与观点的区别，这部分可能使他们更加迷惑。） 辨别事实与观点是思辨的基础，但是在现实中，有时并不易区分两者，因为有一些陈述以事实的面目出现，但它们可能并非事实。因此，学生应学会审辨逻辑链中的每一环。 A. 让学生审视左侧两个句子：究竟是事实还是观点？ B. 第一句显然不是事实。说话人的目的很可能只是为了说明鲁迅先生的文学造诣和地位。如果是这样，怎样将其修改成已提供了有力佐证的事实呢？同理，第二句话在什么情况下可以变成事实呢？引导学生进行讨论。 C. 引导学生审视事实与观点之间的辩证关系。在人们迟疑的地方，或给出不同答案的地方，便值得思考。

Comments/Reflections

1. This activity consists of three phases, during which students are expected to make incremental progress. The exercise in Phase 1 will help students spot the marked difference between facts and opinions through an exercise. In Phase 2, most probably they will realize how scarcely they have based their arguments on hard facts. Phase 3 is intended to help students learn to evaluate the apparent facts more critically and learn how to make effective use of facts.

2. Most students do not realize that there is quite a grey area where it becomes difficult to decide whether a statement is a fact or an opinion. This grey area may be valuable because there are grounds for exploration—questioning, doubting or defending.

3. It is strongly suggested that in Phase 2 the instructor use students' homework as material for discussion. Students will learn more when they realize what they were previously unaware of.

本活动的设计受到以下文献来源的启发: Bozik, Mary. (2001). Fact or Opinion? In Lucas, Stephen E. (ed.) *Selections from the Speech Communication Teacher, 1996–1999*. Madison, Wisconsin: McGraw-Hill. 18–19.

Goal: To promote disciplined interactive thinking that involves collaboration and results in consensus.

Class Size: 40 students or any.

Time: 40 mins.

Pre-Class Reading Assignment: Speaking to Persuade (*APS*, Chapter 14, pp. 192–221).

Materials/Preparation: A. A list of debate topics.

Debate Topics

1. Advertising is harmful.
2. Developed countries should have a higher obligation to environmental protection than developing countries.
3. The government would use torture to obtain information from suspected terrorists.
4. We should ban teachers from interacting with students via social networking Web sites.
5. Newspapers are a thing of the past.

...

B. Sample readings that present opposing views.

Advertising Is Harmful

Pros

- Recent research suggests that people living in a city see up to 5,000 ads every day. Too many advertisements disturb people's everyday life.
- People often feel annoyed when facing too much choice forced by advertisements.
- Advertisements are misleading because companies always present the product as being more effective or more attractive than it really is.
- Advertisements are very bad in sending a message to children that they should have everything they want.
- Advertisements are morally bad because they cause people to keep up with their neighbors on every aspect, which gives rise to jealousy and hate.

...

Cons

- Online advertising alone is believed to be worth $24 billion a year. Almost all public space has advertisements in sight and all forms of media, printed or digital, show that advertising is welcome.
- Advertisements allow ordinary people to make their own choice without turning to experts whom most people have no access to.
- Advertising provides an industry worth billions of dollars across the world.
- Advertising helps companies sell their products, and helps consumers learn what is on offer.
- Advertisements provide people with opportunities to appreciate arts—music, pictures, and animations.

…

C. Groups and positions in each phase (for the instructor's reference).

Phase	Group A		Group B		Group C		Group D		Group E	
	G1	G2	G3	G4	G5	G6	G7	G8	G9	G10
1	Pros	Cons	Pros	Cons	Pros	Cons	Pros	Cons	Pros	Cons
2	Neutral		Neutral		Neutral		Neutral		Neutral	
	Select one best argument from each side of a big group.									
3	Cons	Pros	Cons	Pros	Cons	Pros	Cons	Pros	Cons	Pros
4	Neutral		Neutral		Neutral		Neutral		Neutral	
	Select one best argument.									
5	Neutral		Neutral		Neutral		Neutral		Neutral	
	Present the best argument from each big group.									

PPT/Directions	活动过程描述
1. Forty students. ↓ Five big groups (A, B, C, D, E). ↓ Ten small groups (1, 2; 3, 4; 5, 6; 7, 8; 9, 10).	1. 将全班分成偶数组，每小组四人。不要超过四人，以便每人都有充足的参与时间。相邻两组组成一个大组（如第一和第二组组成A组、第三和第四组组成B组）。大组中的两小组在活动中会充当正反方。（参见 Materials/Preparation C。）
2. Select a topic!	2. 将事先准备好的具有争议性的话题（参见 Materials/Preparation A）给学生，让大家选出最喜欢的一个。假设大家选择了第一个：Advertising Is Harmful。
4. Pros　　　　Cons ↓　　　　　↓ 1, 3, 5, 7, 9　　2, 4, 6, 8, 10	3. 让大家快速阅读教师事先准备好的提示，先激发思维。（这一步为可选，如果学生已有一定的知识储备，则不需要。） 4. 在小组讨论前，分好正反方。所有奇数组为正方，所有偶数组为反方。 （步骤1–4约五分钟。）
5. Phase 1 Small groups. ↓ Select three best arguments.	5. 活动正式进入第一阶段：小组讨论。每人先想出三个最有力的论点，然后将这些论点放在一起进行讨论。讨论中，小组成员需达成一致，挑选出最有力的三个论点。（五分钟。）
6. Phase 2 Big groups. ↓ Select one best argument.	6. 第二阶段（大组活动）：每个大组中配对的正反双方对各自最好的论点进行陈述，大家从中选出最有说服力的一个观点（无论是正方还是反方）。这一环节双方不辩论，只评判论点及论据本身的说服性。 （五分钟。）

（待续）

PPT/Directions	活动过程描述
7. **Phase 3** (Switch positions.) A. Pros → 2, 4, 6, 8, 10 Cons → 1, 3, 5, 7, 9 B–C. Small groups. ↓ Select three best arguments.	7. 第三阶段：第二轮小组讨论。 A. 正反双方交换位置，原来的正方需辩反方观点，而原来的反方则需辩正方观点。 B. 这一环节中，鼓励大家增加新的论据或论证角度。 C. 小组成员再次汇集各自的有力论证，并达成一致，挑选出最好的三项。 （五分钟。）
8. **Phase 4** Big groups. ↓ Select one best argument. ↓ Be an independent, open-minded, and critical thinker!	8. 第四阶段：第二轮大组活动。正反两个小组重新汇合，将上一环节产生的最佳论证展示出来。此时，双方全部放弃自己原来的立场，仅基于论证本身的逻辑性与内容细节，大组讨论与协商，达成一致，挑选出一个最佳论证。 （五分钟。） （在每次大组活动之前，教师提醒学生判断的依据应为论证本身，不受个人情感因素影响。）
9. **Phase 5** Class report.	9. 第五阶段：班级汇报。各大组派代表对最有利的论证进行一分钟陈述。 （五分钟。）
Extended Procedure	**拓展活动**
10–11 Defend the best argument! ↓ Writing is thinking.	10. 第一种拓展活动为上一阶段的继续，即各大组陈述之后，由教师组织，全班讨论和协商，挑选出最具说服力的一项论证。学生应讨论投票的依据。 11. 第二种拓展活动为课后写作任务：每位学生需选择一方观点，进行一篇演讲（constructive speech）。

1. This activity can well apply to classes of any size, although the procedure presented here is designed for a class of 40 students.

2. The goal of the activity is to develop students' critical thinking skills by allowing them an opportunity to discuss a controversial topic through structured design. Students would be very excited (though not very used to this practice) about switching positions and arguing against what they have previously defended. However, this is precisely what the activity is aimed—to teach them how to think in others' positions and therefore achieve a comparatively impartial view of an issue.

3. In fact, this activity is not to teach students what to think but how to think!

4. An interesting thing about this activity is that the instructor remains almost a bystander, leaving all the procedure going among the groups—big and small. The only thing the instructor should watch closely is that every student is engaged and excited.

5. Materials provided are only samples. It is encouraged that the instructor can choose current controversial topics.

本活动的设计基于以下文献来源：Koehler, Carol. (2001). Using Collaborative Controversy in the Critical Thinking Classroom. In Lucas, Stephen E. (ed.) *Selections from the Speech Communication Teacher, 1996–1999*. Madison, Wisconsin: McGraw-Hill. 19–20.

Organization and Outlining

13

UNIT

UNDERSTANDING TEACHING

No man can reveal to you aught but that which already lies half asleep in the dawning of your knowledge. The instructor who walks in the shadow of the temple, among his followers, gives not of his wisdom but rather of his faith and his lovingness. If he is indeed wise he does not bid you enter the house of his wisdom, but rather leads you to the threshold of your own mind.

—Kahlil Gibran

TEACHER' GUIDE (Q & A)

➤ **什么是"组织（organization）"与"提纲制订（outlining）"？**

- 遵循一定的认知规律，将演讲内容按照一定的顺序串联起来，这种顺序原则便是内容的组织方式；将这种串联过程中的关键环节列出来，这便是制订提纲。
- 提纲以简洁的书面文字形式呈现演讲内容框架中的关键环节，并指示各环节之间的逻辑链接。

➤ **该教学环节何时进行？**

- 《演讲的艺术》第十版（中国版）教材中，该环节集中安排在：
  A. Organizing the Body of the Speech (*APS*, Chapter 7, pp. 88–101)；
  B. Beginning and Ending the Speech (*APS*, Chapter 8, pp. 102–117)；
  C. Outlining the Speech (*APS*, Chapter 9, pp. 118–129)；
  D. Types of Informative Speeches: Analysis and Organization (*APS*, Chapter 13, pp. 177–184)；
  E. Persuasive Speeches on Questions of Fact, Persuasive Speeches on Questions of Value, Persuasive Speeches on Questions of Policy (*APS*, Chapter 14, pp. 195–204).
- 该教学环节可在上述任何一部分进行，也可在评价学生演讲稿时进行。

➤ 该教学环节有何必要性?

- 演讲的内容组织和提纲制订犹如给整个演讲搭框架,以确定内容各环节之间的逻辑关系,其重要性不言而喻。
- 演讲作为交流艺术,要求信息传递的清晰性。而信息交流的清晰度从演讲者和听众两方面均依赖于清晰的组织结构。
- 演讲的组织方式,与演讲的其他三个要素——内容(idea)、语言(language)、演讲表达(delivery)相比较,最有规律可循,最易掌握,也有利于从宏观上把握演讲的全局结构,因此可作为最基本的知识来掌握。

➤ 该环节的主要教学目标是什么?

- 培养学生演讲时中心明确、条理清晰的思维习惯。
- 帮助学生了解演讲的开篇(introduction)、主体(body)和结尾(conclusion)的功能与表现形式。
- 帮助学生掌握一般的以及针对不同类型演讲的组织方法。包括时间顺序(chronological order)、空间顺序(spatial order)、话题顺序(topical order)、问题—出路顺序(problem-solution order)、比较优势顺序(comparison advantage order)、门罗动机序列(Monroe's motivated sequence)等。
- 帮助学生掌握英语中逻辑连贯的语言体现方式,特别是段落之间、句子之间以及小句之间的各种连接手段(connectives)。

➤ 常见的教学困难

- 如何唤醒和提高学生对提纲重要性的认识?
- 如何让提纲真正反映演讲的内部逻辑关系?

➤ 教与学的误区

- 讲稿写作之前的提纲写作,在实践中非必有环节。
- 在脑中构思提纲与书写提纲的功效等同。
- 写作提纲很简单,即给出一个核心观点,列出两三个分论点即可。

The PREP Format: Four Simple Steps to a Clear Presentation

Goal: To provide beginning students with an easily remembered format for constructing a one-minute presentation.

Class Size: Up to 40 students.

Time: 20–25 mins.

Pre-Class Reading Assignment:
A. Organizing the Body of the Speech (*APS*, Chapter 7, pp. 88–101).
B. Outlining the Speech (*APS*, Chapter 9, pp. 118–129).

Materials/Preparation:
A. The PREP Format.

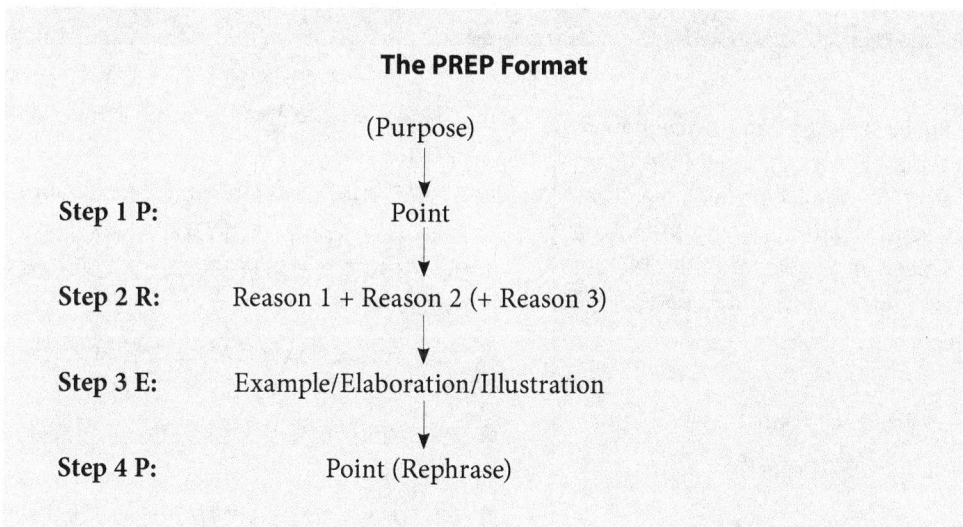

The PREP Format

(Purpose)
↓
Step 1 P: Point
↓
Step 2 R: Reason 1 + Reason 2 (+ Reason 3)
↓
Step 3 E: Example/Elaboration/Illustration
↓
Step 4 P: Point (Rephrase)

B. Topic cards.

Topic Card 1

1. What is the most important when preparing for an examination?
2. What is the most important when choosing a mobile phone?
3. What is the most important when making friends?

Topic Card 2

1. My happiest memory.
2. One of my most embarrassing memories.
3. My favorite book.

Topic Card 3

1. There are two/three steps in making… (e.g., a meal).
2. There are two/three don'ts in shopping online.
3. There are two things to do to alleviate anxiety.

Topic Card 4

What do the quotes mean?

1. The way to gain a good reputation is to endeavor to be what you desire to appear. —Socrates
2. An honest man is always a child. —Socrates
3. Charity begins at home. —Proverb

In-Class Procedure

PPT/Directions	活动过程描述
1–2 *Directions:* Public speaking can be a nightmare to many people. However, when we learn certain strategies, it won't be a nightmare any more. In this activity, you are going to make a one-minute speech on a choice of three different topics. Try to follow the PREP pattern of organization. The PREP Format (Purpose) ↓ Step 1 P:　　　Point ↓ Step 2 R: Reason 1 + Reason 2 (+ Reason 3) ↓ Step 3 E: Example/Elaboration/Illustration ↓ Step 4 P:　　Point (Rephrase)	1. 向学生交代，这项活动的主要任务是"一分钟演讲"。遵循一定的组织策略，一分钟演讲将不再是可怕的事情。 2. 向学生解释本项活动所介绍的组织策略——PREP 模式，即"观点—理由—阐述/解释—观点总结"四个步骤。将 PREP 模式展示于屏幕上，让学生直观地了解四个步骤。 第一步，在确定好演讲目的之后，也就是针对题目中要求回答的问题，先给出一个主要观点。 第二步，给出持此观点的主要理由，可以只有一个，也可以有两三个。 第三步，对每一个理由，均需给出进一步的介绍或阐释。如果只有一个理由，则需要给出较为详尽的解释。 第四步，最后对主要观点进行总结和强调。 （这个环节的时间约三分钟。）

（待续）

PPT/Directions	活动过程描述
	3. 将事先准备好的四张话题卡（参见 Materials/Preparation B）分发给不同的小组（每组以不超过六人为宜）。如果班上超过四个小组，则有些小组拿到相同的话题卡。
4. **Notes** P: _____ R1: _____ 　E1: _____ 　E2: _____ R2: _____ 　E1: _____ 　E2: _____ P: _____	4. 小组成员从话题卡上的三个话题中选出自己喜欢的一个。根据PREP四个步骤，每位同学做笔记，准备自己的演讲。准备时间为一分半钟，可以讨论。 准备期间，可参照左侧笔记框架进行准备（也可以按照自己的想法做）。做笔记可用记录关键词或符号的方式，不要将整个句子都写下来。 初学者可尝试根据笔记组织演讲，每一行为一个句子。八句话在一分钟之内说完，既不会感觉太空荡，也不会出现时间不够的情况。每个人语速有差异，究竟一分钟大致可以完成几句话？多少单词？这些需要学生在实践中不断总结经验。
5–7 Speak to the Group ↓ Speak to the Whole Class ↓ Q & A 7. | Speech	Questions
Group 1	Groups 2 & 3
Group 2	Groups 3 & 4
Group 3	Groups 4 & 1
Group 4	Groups 1 & 2		5. 一分半钟之后，所有同学停止准备。由小组长组织，每人依次进行一分钟陈述。 （准备及小组内陈述的时间总共不超过九分钟。） 6. 小组陈述完毕，推选出最佳的一组，依次在全班进行一分钟演讲。 7. 一分钟演讲结束之后，由其他小组提两个问题。教师应协调提问机会，尽量给各小组均等的参与机会（例如左侧所示的问答顺序）。每个问题的回答时间不超过20秒钟。必要时，教师应予以提示。 如果班里超过五组，则这次活动只需要四个小组推选演讲，其余小组则主要承担提问任务。（约10分钟。） 8. 全班投票选出演讲和回答问题综合评价最好的一组。（教师可以考虑给予不同形式的奖励或鼓励。）

Comments/Reflections

1. This activity is designed for beginning public speakers to learn to fill up the duration of one minute with a well-organized speech. Novice speakers often find that they have nothing else to say after responding to the topic with a brief one-sentence answer. The PREP format helps students extend that one sentence to about eight sentences in a logical way. The format is like the ABC of public speaking for all Chinese students.

2. Attention should be paid to two important details. First, make sure that everybody gets at least two "Rs" (reasons) or otherwise at least two "Es" (examples). Second, make sure that students have more to say than time allows them to. For example, if you find it still hard for them to speak continuously for one minute, instead of allowing for more preparation time, limit the speaking time to 40 seconds, or the responding time to 10 or 15 seconds. The trick here is to give them a feeling that they can still speak more if time allows.

3. As students progress, more things should be considered. For example, does the point forcefully respond to the topic? Do the Es logically connect to the R(s)?

4. In a small class, try to give each student a chance to speak.

Goal: Through a relay game, to teach students how to apply conventions of organization and outlining in a real-life speaking situation.

Class Size: Ideally 40 students.

Time: 35 mins.

Pre-Class Reading Assignment:
A. Organizing the Body of the Speech (*APS*, Chapter 7, pp. 88–101).
B. Beginning and Ending the Speech (*APS*, Chapter 8, pp. 102–117).
C. Outlining the Speech (*APS*, Chapter 9, pp. 118–129).

Materials/Preparation:
A. Arrow Through Ass' Ribs Outline Form. (Spare copies may be needed.)

Arrow Through Ass' Ribs Outline Form	
Introduction	**Criteria for Evaluation**
A: Attention strategy	Unique/interesting
R: Relate topic to audience	Build interest/general purpose (Issue development)
R: Relate topic to self	Establish credibility
O: Oratorical purpose (Purpose of communication)	Clear and succinct central idea and purpose sentence
W: What you are going to say	Clear and succinct preview
Body	
A: Assertion (Sub-point 1)	Full sentence supporting thesis
S: Supporting details	Relevant, strong evidence
S: Supporting details	Cite source or reference
(Transition/Internal summary)	
A: Assertion (Sub-point 2)	
S: Supporting details	
S: Supporting details	
(Transition/Internal summary)	
A: Assertion (Sub-point 1)	
S: Supporting details	

（待续）

Arrow Through Ass' Ribs Outline Form	
S: Supporting details	
Conclusion	
R: Review	Preview in past tense
I: Instruct audience	(Expanded when necessary)
B: Bonder (Bond it with a brief anecdote or quote)	Last statement/illustrate/quote
S: Solicit questions	
Delivery: _____Volume _____Articulation _____Force _____Eye Contact	
_____Visual Aids _____Language	

B. Sequence order of speaking.

Sequence Number	Content	Speaker
	Introduction	
1	**A:** Attention strategy	Speaker 1 (1–3)
2	**R:** Relate topic to audience	
3	**R:** Relate topic to self	
4	**O:** Oratorical purpose (Purpose of communication)	Speaker 2 (4 & 5)
5	**W:** What you are going to say	
	Body	
6	**A:** Assertion (Sub-point 1)	Speaker 3 (6–8)
7	S: Supporting details	
8	S: Supporting details	
9	(Transition/Internal summary)	Speaker 4 (9)
10	**A:** Assertion (Sub-point 2)	Speaker 5 (10–12)
11	S: Supporting details	
12	S: Supporting details	
13	(Transition/Internal summary)	Speaker 6 (13)
14	**A:** Assertion (Sub-point 3)	Speaker 7 (14–16)
15	S: Supporting details	
16	S: Supporting details	
	Conclusion	
17	**R:** Review	Speaker 8 (17)

（待续）

Sequence Number	Content	Speaker
18	**I**: Instruct audience	Speaker 9 (18)
19	**B**: Bonder (Bond it with a brief anecdote or quote)	Speaker 10 (19 & 20)
20	**S**: Solicit questions	

C. Topic cards. Choose one of the topics for this activity.

Topic Card 1

(an informative speech)

Your university is going to celebrate its …th anniversary. You are going to make a speech on behalf of the student union on its brilliant history.

Topic Card 2

(a persuasive speech)

Plastic surgery is often seen as a self-confidence booster. However, it might be harmful. Make a speech under this title:

Plastic Surgery Should Not Be Encouraged Among University Students

In-Class Procedure

PPT/Directions	活动过程描述
1. Briefing Introduction to the Pattern ↓ Group Discussion (six mins.) ↓ Speaking Relay 1 (up to four mins.) ↓ Speaking Relay 2 (up to four mins.) ↓ Comments and Votes	1. 向学生介绍本次活动的主要目的及程序： 目的：熟悉一个较为完整的演讲线索及演讲的一般组织形式； 程序： A. 熟悉这一较为"万能"的演讲组织框架； B. 小组对给定题目进行讨论（六分钟）； C. 两个大组进行演讲接力赛，即小组的每个成员完成一至两句话，并最终组成一个完整的演讲（各四分钟）； D. 点评及评选获胜队。 （如左侧幻灯片所示。）

（待续）

PPT/Directions	活动过程描述

2.
 	
ARROW-ASS-RIBS
 	
Introduction: ARROW
Body:
  A1-SS
  A2-SS
  A3-SS
Conclusion: RIBS
	2. 向学生介绍 Arrow Through Ass' Ribs Outline Form（参见 Materials/Preparation A）。将该组织模式展示于屏幕上。提醒学生，该结构与《演讲的艺术》第126–127页上 Sample Speaking Outline 相一致。
	
	　A. 将此线索从头至尾粗略顺一遍，包括组成部分及评估标准。
	
	　B. 强调框架中最核心的部分，即该模式的缩略版（如左侧幻灯片所示）。

3. Guide for Preparation (six mins.) Step 1: Decide the specific purpose and central idea. Step 2: Decide the three sub-points. Step 3: Decide the supporting details. Step 4: Discuss the opening and closing parts. Step 5: Allow a minute for everybody to rehearse.	3. 将全班分为四大组，每组10人。发给每组相同的题目（参见 Materials/Preparation C，选择一题）。告诉学生他们将在讨论之后进行小组演讲接力，每名同学均需参与。将演讲顺序表（参见 Materials/Preparation B）展示于屏幕。 将事先准备好的材料A的复印件分发给小组，最好3–4人能共享一份，以作参照。 提醒大家，材料A表中第一列所标的每一个序号，其所对应的内容最好控制在一句话。小组分配角色。 建议小组讨论遵循左侧幻灯片所示的线索。
4–6 Finding two speaking teams and two judging teams. ↓ Speaking Relay 1. ↓ Speaking Relay 2.	4. 讨论结束，用抽签的方式决定两个参加演讲接力赛的小组。 5. 其他两个小组则分别担任评委，一组负责一场演讲。需要有计时员，在每分钟时间到时提醒演讲小组。其他组员则参照材料A中的评估标准对演讲进行记录，准备随后的点评。教师分发材料A复印件，保证两人共看一份标准。 6. 第一组演讲接力赛开始。按照事先排好的顺序，每位成员依次演讲。 7. 第二组演讲接力赛开始。按照事先排好的顺序，每位成员依次演讲。
8. Guide for Evaluation (two mins. for each group) • Duration? • Engagement? • Introduction? • Body? • Conclusion? • Delivery? • Language?	8. 两个点评小组分别对比赛小组进行点评（两分钟）。教师可引导点评小组进行类似的点评接力，即分散任务，使尽量多的学生有机会发表见解。将点评提示展示在屏幕上，但不要求学生严格遵守该顺序。 9. 全班投票选出获胜的演讲接力组。

1. Students would find this activity challenging yet exciting. The challenge lies not only in speaking itself but also that the speaker has to incorporate his own role into the team work. Consequently, the evaluation would focus on two things: whether the speaker fulfilled his or her role of speaking; and whether the speech contributed to the coherence of the whole speech.

2. To ensure that the speaking procedure goes smoothly, the instructor should make sure that group discussion is well done. The group has to work together and decide together about the main sub-points, supporting details and other details. Students should easily notice that the workload for each role is not equal. This is so designed as to allow each student comfortably participate in the relay—confident people may take up "heavy" work and less confident ones may take up easier work.

3. The main purpose of the activity is to familiarize everybody with the general organization pattern of a speech, so be lenient if the logic is somewhat loose or that the loopholes are spotted in the details. But the instructor should remind students of logical problems.

4. An even more challenging adaptation of the activity would be that the speech is given alternatively by two groups, with one person from Group A speaking first and one from Group B next, and then the relay baton going back to Group A... In this case each speaker has to struggle fitting into the logic of the whole speech.

本活动的设计基于以下文献来源：[1] Gschwend, Laura L. (1998). Outlining Relay. In Lucas, Stephen E. (ed.) *Selections from the Speech Communication Teacher, 1994–1996*. Madison, Wisconsin: McGraw-Hill. 52–53. [2] Ensign, Russell L. (1995). The "Arrow Through Ass' Ribs" Outline: A Teaching Aid for the Basic Course. In Lucas, Stephen E. (ed.) *Selections from the Speech Communication Teacher, 1991–1994*. Madison, Wisconsin: McGraw-Hill. 45–46.

Language & Style

UNDERSTANDING TEACHING

I'm not a teacher: only a fellow traveler of whom you asked the way. I pointed ahead—ahead of myself as well as you.

—*George Bernard Shaw*

You persuade a man only insofar as you can talk his language by speech, gesture, tonality, order, image, attitude, idea, identifying your ways with his.

—*Kenneth Burke*

The classroom should be what it is trying to foster.

—*Eliot Eisner*

TEACHER'S GUIDE (Q & A)

➤ **演讲中的"语言及语言风格"指什么?**

- 英语演讲中的语言使用至少包括两个维度：一是语言的准确、清晰和生动；二是恰当的语言风格。

- 第一个维度即为人们通常所说的遣词造句以及文法规范。从语言学角度说，主要是词汇、句法的运用以及语篇连贯的处理。第二个维度要求文体风格适合演讲场合、受众品味、话题以及演讲者的身份等。从语言学角度说，属于语用或语域范畴。两个维度均涉及修辞的运用。

➤ **该教学环节何时进行?**

- 在《演讲的艺术》第十版（中国版）教材中，该环节集中安排在第十章"语言使用"(Using Language, *APS*, Chapter 10, pp. 130–144)。

- 该环节的教学可在 *APS* 教材第十章集中进行，也可在学生的演讲稿出现较为集中的语言问题时进行。

➤ **该教学环节有何必要性?**

- 所有精彩的内容最终都需以语言的形式来体现。从某种程度上讲，演讲的冲击力源自语言的魅力。

- 大学生的英语能力本身就有待于提高，故在演讲准备中语言的组织与提炼显得尤为重要。

➤ 该环节的主要教学目标及内容是什么?

- 帮助学生了解英语书面语、半书面语、口语之间的差别，培养学生英语运用中的交流意识，学会"对什么人说什么话"。
- 帮助学生了解英语演讲语言风格的一般原则，如：
  - 使用清晰、简洁的语言；
  - 使用生动、描述性的词汇；
  - 使用地道的英语表达；
  - 避免过于口语化的语言；
  - 避免过于抽象的描述或论证；
  - 避免俚语、行话或任何冒犯性的语言等。
- 帮助学生了解和掌握各种英语修辞格，提高信息传递的有效性，特别注意运用语音、句法和语义层面上的重复、类比与对比等各种修辞格，增强演讲效果。
  演讲中常用的修辞格包括：排比（parallelism）、对偶（antithesis）、头韵（alliteration）、明喻（simile）、隐喻（metaphor）、借代（synecdoche/metonymy）、拟人（personification）、双关（pun）、夸张（hyperbole）、矛盾修饰法（oxymoron）、反语（irony）、反问（rhetorical question）、拟声（onomatopoeia）等。
- 帮助学生学会使用个性化语言，增加演讲者的可信度，突显演讲者的身份特征，提高与公众交流的效果。

➤ 常见的教学困难

- 英语对中国学生来说是一门外语，学生的英语语言能力薄弱，常不能满足演讲的要求。因此，英语演讲课教学常需要兼顾外语能力与演讲能力的同步提高。
- 修辞格的运用对语言能力要求很高，需要学生对语音、词汇、语法等语言三大要素均有较为娴熟的掌握。由于大部分学生的语言积累仍有欠缺，因此教学难度加大。
- 英语演讲的教学内容多，任务重，能够分配给语言这一章节的教学时间非常有限，很难有所突破或提高。

➤ 教与学的误区

- 英语演讲的语言风格就是日常交流口语的风格，即采用非正式语体。正式语体主要用于书面作品。
- 成功的英语演讲也主要依赖于流利的口语，语言质量本身并不重要。
- 绝大多数中国大学生目前英语水平还不能达到演讲的要求，因此语言上不要严格要求。
- 如果找不到一种能使学生的语言能力在半年内有明显提高的教学方法，就等于语言教学没有效果。

14.1 Powerspeak: Avoiding Ambiguous Language

Goal:	To make students aware of the ineffectiveness and inaccuracies of ambiguous language so that they can adapt their messages for clarity and preciseness.
Class Size:	Any.
Time:	10–15 mins.
Pre-Class Reading Assignment:	Using Language Accurately, Using Language Clearly (*APS*, Chapter 10, pp. 131–135).
Materials/Preparation:	Abstraction Language Questionnaire.

Abstraction Language Questionnaire

Directions: Read each question carefully. Then write down your **first response** to the question. Your answer is based on your interpretation of the bold-faced words.

1. Li Qiang just graduated from college and is making a **good** salary. How much does he make per year?
2. Wang Fang just graduated from college and is making **a lot** of money. How much does she make per year?
3. Anthony is **short**. How tall is Anthony?
4. Mr. Mills came **late** to the reception that was to begin at three o'clock. What time did he arrive?
5. The man is **big**. How much does the man weigh?
6. John is **old**. How old is John?
7. Mary is **elderly**. How old is Mary?
8. You are reading an **old** book. What is the publication date?
9. You have a **long** commute to school. How many kilometers do you travel?
10. Bob has been absent from class **a lot**. How many days has he missed?

⏱ In-Class Procedure

PPT/Directions	活动过程描述
1–2 Questionnaire ↑ What's your first response?	1. 将问卷（参见Materials/Preparation）分发给每一位同学。 2. 让学生独立完成问卷。需要强调"第一反应"。(五分钟。)
3–5 Six Volunteers ↓ Surprise—Different Answers!	3. 邀请六位自愿者上台跟大家分享自己的答案。六位自愿者的性别分布尽可能均匀。 4. 自愿者面对全班同学，手里拿着自己完成的问卷。 5. 从第一个问题问起，要求六位自愿者依次报出自己的答案。一般情况下，六个答案会有较大差异，特别是涉及性别、文化和年龄等领域。
6. Clear and Precise Language • Immediately comprehensible meaning • No chance of misunderstanding • Familiar, concrete words	6. 引导学生了解"语言的准确性、清晰性"的含义。演讲的语言应尽量不使听众产生误解或迷惑。

Comments/Reflections

1. Clear and precise language is important to smooth communication with a big audience. Speaking with specificity will help the audience picture an image that is similar to that of the speaker's meaning. In contrast, ambiguous language forces the audience to use their own frame of reference to serve as an anchor that interprets the ambiguous phrase into a more specific message. This is where disparity is created.

2. This is a very interesting mini-activity. Students will instantly realize what ambiguous language means; more importantly, they will listen for and criticize those who continue to use such language.

本活动的设计来源于以下文献：Zizik, Catherine H. (1998). Powerspeak: Avoiding Ambiguous Language. In Lucas, Stephen E. (ed.) *Selections from the Speech Communication Teacher, 1994–1996*. Madison, Wisconsin: McGraw-Hill. 44–45.

Goal:	To teach students how to compose single, double, and AB-BA antithetic statements.
Class Size:	Any.
Time:	15–20 mins.
Pre-Class Reading Assignment:	Using Language Vividly (*APS*, Chapter 10, pp. 135–139).
Materials/Preparation:	A. Examples of single antithesis.

Examples of Single Antithesis

One antonym on each side of the seesaw.

Quotes:

- Give me *liberty*—or give me *death*. —Patrick Henry
- *Actions*! Not *words*! —Def Leppard

From American students:

- You can't be *happy*, if you make others *sad*.
- Talking *a lot* may express so *little*.

B.   Example of double antithesis.

Examples of Double Antithesis

Two antonyms on each side of the seesaw.

Quotes:

- That's one *small step* for a *man*, one *giant leap* for *mankind*. —Neil Armstrong
- If a free society cannot help the *many* who are *poor* it cannot save the *few* who are *rich*. —John Kennedy
- There are *so many* things that we wish we had done *yesterday*, *so few* that we feel like doing *today*. —Mignon McLaughlin
- *Man proposes, God disposes*. —Proverb
- To *err* is *human*, to *forgive*, *divine*. —Alexander Pope

From American students:

- *Burning* is the *hot sun*; *frigid* is the *cold snow*.
- With *life* comes *questions*; with *death* comes the *final answer*.
- The *first* time we *quarreled* was the *last* time we *spoke*.
- *Love* cleans *a bad man's heart*, but *hatred* stains *a good man's soul*.

C. Examples of AB–BA antithesis.

Examples of AB–BA Antithesis

The AB-BA pattern.

Quotes:

- Let's never *negotiate* out of *fear*, but let us never *fear* to *negotiate*. —John Kennedy

From advertisements:

- Pan Am *flies* the *world* the way the *world* wants to *fly*.
- You can take *Salem* out of the *country*, but you can't take the *country* out of *Salem*.

From American students:

- It is better to *fear life* than to live a *life* of *fear*.
- It is *fun* to *learn* what you *learn* for *fun*.
- You must *control* your *emotions* or your *emotions* will *control* you.

In-Class Procedure

PPT/Directions	活动过程描述
1. Three steps to antithesis.	1. 对偶是演讲中最常用的修辞手法之一，但对学生来说也是最困难的。这个活动将分三个步骤来教授学生对偶的几种形式。
2. Single Antithesis _____ — _____ ↓ ___liberty___ — ___death___ ↓ Give me *liberty*—or give me *death.*	2. 第一步，单对偶。 A. 学生两人一组准备活动。在纸上画出左右两条相对的线。 B. 分别在两条线上写下一对反义词。 C. 用这对反义词组成一句话。 鼓励学生开动脑筋，积极思考。如果学生一时想不出来，可以使用材料A中的例句进行提示。
3. Double Antithesis A. To *err* is *human*, to *forgive*, *divine.* err vs. forgive human vs. divine	3. 第二步，复对偶。 A. 先示范一个名言的例子（参见Materials/Preparation B）。

（待续）

PPT/Directions	活动过程描述
B–C life vs. death love vs. hate first vs. last heart vs. soul white vs. black man vs. god question vs. answer … ↓ With *life* comes *questions*; with *death* comes the *final* answer.	B. 让学生先罗列所能想到的互为反义词的词对。 C. 从这些反义词对中，挑选两组，按照范例形式造句。 可以继续使用材料B中的例句提示学生，然后再让学生创造出自己的对偶句。 Materials/Preparation B中提供的例子可以作为讲解例句，也可以用来给学生进行提示。
4. AB-BA Antithesis A. Let's never *negotiate* out of *fear*, but let us never *fear* to *negotiate*. negotiate fear fear negotiate A B B A	4. 第三步，顶针对偶。 A. 先例示顶针对偶（参见 Materials/Preparation C）。 B. 将材料C分发给各小组，让学生小组讨论（这部分时间为三分钟），并造出自己的顶针对偶句。可用美国学生造的句子启发和鼓励学生。 C. 各组汇报、分享自己的成果。

Comments/Reflections

1. Antithesis is one of the most frequently used figures of speech in public speaking, so students really need to acquire the use of it.

2. Students are most probably intimidated by the very term "antithesis" or its use in "Let's never *negotiate* out of *fear*, but let us never *fear* to *negotiate*" at first sight. This is even daunting for American college students. So the instructor's encouragement and facilitation would be vitally important. When they do eventually rise to the occasion and even excel at the end of the task a sense of pride forms in the groups.

3. This activity allows students to conquer such difficulty step by step. After all, they can make their own simple antithesis, and then, the double and AB-BA antithesis won't seem far away.

4. The lists of examples in Materials/Preparation are provided for flexible use—as examples, prompts, or reading materials.

本活动的设计基于以下文献：Zizik, Catherine H. (1998). Powerspeak: Avoiding Ambiguous Language. In Lucas, Stephen E. (ed.) *Selections from the Speech Communication Teacher, 1994–1996*. Madison, Wisconsin: McGraw-Hill. 44–45.

Visual Aids

UNDERSTANDING TEACHING

Use technology with me, I'll participate, I'll transfer, I'll employ, and I'll create.

—*Tony Erben, Ruth Ban & Martha Castaneda*

A good instructor, like a good entertainer, first must hold his audience's attention, then he can teach his lesson.

—*John Henrik Clarke*

An instructor should have maximal authority, and minimal power.

—*Thomas Szasz*

TEACHER'S GUIDE (Q & A)

➤ **视觉辅助物（visual aids）包括哪些?**

- 视觉辅助物是指任何用于说明和解释演讲内容的、需要受众视觉感知的实体。视觉辅助物形式多样，可包括：物品及模型（objects and models）、照片和图画（photographs and drawings）、图解（graphs）、图表（charts）、视频（video）、演讲者（the speaker）以及演示文稿（PowerPoint，PPT）。
- 目前使用最广泛的视觉辅助物为PPT。

➤ **该教学环节何时进行?**

- 在《演讲的艺术》第十版（中国版）教材中，该环节集中安排在第十二章"巧用视觉辅助物"（Using Visual Aids, *APS*, Chapter 12, pp. 160–175)。
- 实际的教学操作可灵活安排。可以在学生之前的演讲实践中零星涉及，或在第十二章中集中讲解；可以将本章内容直接分解到平时的演讲实践和讲解讨论中；也可以引导学生及时将所学的相关知识总结成"检查清单（checklist）"，并不断完善。
- 《演讲的艺术》教师用书所提供的DVD中"Speeches for Analysis and Discussion"部分，有三个演讲实例（"Pot, Soil, Water"、"Securing Yourself Online"、"The Hidden World of Chili Peppers"），分别提供了Need-Improvement Version和Final Version。这几个实例非常适合例示视觉辅助物的使用原则。

➤ **该教学环节有何必要性?**

- 视觉辅助物在真实情景的演讲中几乎不可或缺,是演讲的重要组成部分。
- 人们对视觉辅助物的种类以及PPT的使用仍存在误解,因此教学非常必要。

➤ **该环节的主要教学目标是什么?**

- 帮助学生了解视觉辅助物与演讲之间的关系以及对演讲的作用。
- 帮助学生了解不同种类的视觉辅助物的使用场合。
- 帮助学生重点了解PPT的使用原则,包括信息容量、字体字号处理、色彩选择、其他版面设计以及动画制作要点等。

➤ **视觉辅助物的使用应遵循什么原则?**

- 视觉辅助物应该简洁,所传递的信息或含义应一目了然。
- 视觉辅助物的量需恰到好处,不易滥用。主要用于关键信息,或用于对信息递送比文字表达更有效时,即有"一幅图抵一千字"的功效时。
- 演讲者需认真对待视觉辅助物。换言之,使用到的视觉辅助物,演讲中一定要提及,否则便不使用;另一方面,演讲没有提及时,视觉辅助物(例如某一页幻灯片或幻灯片的某一部分内容)不提前出现,而这部分内容说完后,则不再展示,以免分散听众注意力。
- 视觉辅助物归根到底是辅助(aid),演讲的焦点应是演讲者。
- 如需使用多媒体等设备,需要提前检查并试用设备,以避免任何可能出现的不测。
- 一定要制订备用计划。万一设备出现故障,演讲仍可正常进行。

➤ **常见的教学误区与困难**

- 教学困难主要在于,需要师生双方克服对视觉辅助物的误解。
- 不少人误认为,视觉辅助物主要就是PPT,公众演讲中,PPT的使用是不可或缺的。此外,在视觉辅助物的使用上,教师和学生易将所有演讲等同于某些场合的口头陈述(oral presentation),如学术会议、产品介绍等。
- 学生过于依赖视觉辅助物,致使辅助喧宾夺主,演讲能力未得到充分训练和展现。
- 学生的PPT设计常出现信息量太大或过于花哨的问题,致使视觉辅助物干扰了主要信息的传递。
- 将大部分信息以文字形式呈现于幻灯片上,演讲蜕变为照本宣科,以致信息递送不奏效。

15.1

Pointing Groups to PowerPoint

Goal: To increase students' understanding, proficiency, and responsible use of PowerPoint.

Class Size: 25–40 students.

Time: Four class meetings, 10 minutes for each of the first three meetings and 40 minutes for the last meeting.

Pre-Class Reading Assignment: None; or Using Visual Aids (*APS*, Chapter 12, pp. 160–175).

Materials/Preparation: A. A sample list of "Organizational Identity."

A List of "Organization Identity"

- Employment Agency
- Mobile Phone Company
- Education Agency
- Health Care Supply Company
- Food Supply Company

B. A guideline for preparation.

Important Details of the Recruitment Plan

- Company name?
- Location of the company?
- Flowchart of power hierarchy?
- Titles for workers?
  Brief description of jobs: qualifications, responsibilities…
- Target candidates

…

C. A record of group progress: members and responsibilities.

Week	Responsibilities	Comments
1	(Who is assigned what job?)	(Problems?)
2		(Fulfillment? Problems?)
3		(Fulfillment? Problems?)
4		(Success/Merits? Failure/Demerits?)

(For students to keep a record of the progress of the group work.)

PPT/Directions	活动过程描述
The First Class Meeting	**第一次课**
1–2 Receive your assignments. *Scenario:* You are going to develop a presentation which communicates to co-workers (the rest of the class) that your organization has grown and will be hiring 100 new employees within the next three months. The members need to collaborate to create a five-minute PPT presentation which communicates this information. Before the finalization of your presentation, you may need to: • Create a company name, titles for workers, location of company and flowchart which indicates the organization's power hierarchy. • Do research and group discussions. Your preparation time is three weeks.	1. 将全班分为五个大组，给每一组分配一个公司类型（Materials/Preparation A中提供了一个样本，可更换）。 2. 小组任务： 公司因为业务发展，在未来三个月内要招收100名员工。小组需要合作，使用PPT完成口头陈述任务，向其他员工（即其他学生）汇报这一信息。小组需要做以下准备： A. 确定公司具体名称、职位名称、公司地点、职位层级分布流程图等。 B. 课后查阅文献并讨论。 任务的准备时间为三个星期。小组可自行细分任务。建议小组使用材料C提供的任务分配与完成表。之后两周的课上都会有10分钟时间进行小结和讨论。 3. 当天课上，主要通过小组协商，确定基本信息，以及任务细节。课后，则需要小组成员查阅资料，各自准备。
The Second Class Meeting	**第二次课**
4. Get all the detailed information.	4. 小组通报信息准备情况，确定整体框架和基本细节。可参见Materials/Preparation中的提示。这一环节既可在小组进行，也可通过小组汇报相互分享。需要完成两项小任务： A. 核查细节信息是否完备？是否还需要课后再落实？ B. 确定PPT框架。课后准备。
The Third Class Meeting	**第三次课**
5. Prepare Your PPT • Number of slides • Highlights • Display	5. 各小组汇报PPT准备情况。包括以下内容： A. 主要线索？几张幻灯片？ B. 以什么方式呈现？ 提醒学生对于五分钟的演讲，幻灯片的张数不宜过多。这一点也可到演讲当日进行检验。 课后需要准备下一次课的五分钟陈述。

（待续）

PPT/Directions	活动过程描述
The Fourth Class Meeting	**第四次课**
6–8 Presentation and reflection. ↓ Smooth? Clear? Effective? Responsible and appropriate use of PPT?	6. 各小组依次进行五分钟的口头陈述，可以派一位代表，也可以是小组合作。 7. 演讲之后，各小组进行自评。然后，其他学生和教师再进行点评。 根据已有教学实践，学生可能出现两个主要问题：第一，幻灯片的张数太多；第二，幻灯片上的文字或图片过多。 8. 书面作业：各小组根据各方意见，书面完成对陈述中PPT使用的自评报告。

Comments/Reflections

1. This is a "big" activity, lasting at least four weeks. It incorporates the use of PPT into the preparation of a speech which requires research too.

2. To ensure smooth progress, the instructor needs to make sure that the tasks for each week are completed. Therefore, a record of group progress: Members and responsibilities (as suggested in Materials/Preparation C), must be kept.

3. Despite the fact that slides are the only visual aids, students usually take great delight in making and appreciating them. So they will have fun.

本活动的设计基于以下文献：Gutgold, Nichola D. (2001). Pointing Groups to PowerPoint. In Lucas, Stephen E. (ed.) *Selections from the Speech Communication Teacher, 1996–1999*. Madison, Wisconsin: McGraw-Hill. 76.

Goal:	To help students draft, update, and finalize a checklist for using PPT for their speech preparation.
Class Size:	Any.
Time:	About three minutes for every class meeting.
Pre-Class Reading Assignment:	Using Visual Aids (*APS*, Chapter 12, pp. 160–175).
Materials/Preparation:	A. A checklist for using PPT (not exhaustive).

A Checklist for Using PPT

- Simple enough? (Too much information?)
  - Never contain every point.
  - Never use complete sentences (except for quotes).
  - Use words or phrases instead.
  - The simpler, the better.
- Large enough? Easily seen?
  - Suggested size: Title: 44; Subtitle: 36; Other text: 28.
- Fonts
  - Easy to read?
  - A limited number? (≤ 3)
  - Consistent use?
- Text
  - More than six lines? (≤ 6)
- Color
  - Easy to read?

  (Note: The display on your computer is not the same as that on the big screen! Check before the speech day!)
  - A limited number of colors? (≤ 3; background, title, text)
  - Consistent use of colors?
- Images
  - Truly necessary?
  - Large, clear and simple enough?
  - A title above?
  - Video properly edited and timed?
  - Copyright information included?
- Space
  - A pleasing sense of visual balance?

- Animation
  - Distractive?
  - Lines displayed before they are discussed?
  (Note: Don't display everything at once! Display when you come to it!)
- Language
  - Spelling? Grammar?
  - Consistence of capitalization? Punctuation?

(A final note: Save your file in a format that the computer in the classroom can open.)

B. Top problems with PPT.

Top Problems with PPT

- Overwhelming text information.
- Overwhelming pictures.
- Improper background color which makes it hard to read.
- Language errors.

…

C. Two video clips:
a) "Secure Yourself Online";
b) "The Hidden World of Chili Peppers."
Both provide a version in need of improvement and an improved version. The instructor may use them for comparison when necessary (taken from *APS Teacher's Manual, Speeches for Analysis and Discussion, DVD*).

In-Class Procedure

PPT/Directions	活动过程描述
1–2 Something wrong with my PPT? The principles?	1. 在准备第一次演讲时，要求需要制作PPT的学生课外浏览教材第十二章。每次课上对演讲实践进行点评时，引导学生关注PPT的制作和演示（如果使用的话）。 2. 在班上找一位自愿者（或指派一位学生），负责对讨论中提到的PPT的使用原则进行记录和整理，制作PPT使用的检查清单。该清单并不是一次性完成，而是每次补充，最后完善。

（待续）

PPT/Directions	活动过程描述

3–5
 	
Noticed these problems before?
 	
"Let's make our own checklist!"
	3. 为了不占用太多上课时间（约一两分钟或两三分钟），教师可引导学生先关注最明显的问题。例如：
	
	  A. 最容易犯的错误就是，幻灯片上满是文字或图片，导致听众只看PPT，而不去关注演讲人。
	
	  B. 未采用动画方式逐条播放，而是一次性将所有信息全部展现在幻灯片上，造成听众迷惑或分散注意力。
	
	  （可参照但不局限于Materials/Preparation B。）
	
	4. 之后，每次课上遇到有使用PPT的情况时，有针对性地讨论两三个小问题，以加深记忆。
	
	5. 负责记录的学生每次课后对检查清单进行整理，并发送至班级邮箱或上传至共享平台，以供所有学生随时参照。

6. Effective use of PPT. No abuse of it!	6. 在检查清单基本补充完善后，请负责记录的学生为全班进行一次"PPT使用原则"的微型讲座，可参考Materials/Preparation A。 （五分钟左右。） 教师在整个活动过程中应该时刻提醒学生：有效利用PPT；不滥用PPT。

Comments/Reflections

1. Unlike most of the other activities which are done in one class period, this one requires continuous engagement. This is because students simply cannot learn the principles for using PPT within the duration of 40 minutes—even though the theory can be imparted, many parts of it won't leave a mark on students' brains. Students need experiences as a speaker as well as an audience to understand the problems and the solutions. It would also be a pleasant experience to complete their checklist for using PPT based on their own analysis and reflections.

2. Most students don't feel that it's a big problem to contain overwhelming information or pictures in the slides, nor do they see anything wrong with reading aloud from the text or allow the audience to read from the text displayed on the screen. So, it is important to tell students that in a speech class the speaker and his or her speech should always be the focus of attention. Although the inclusion of a full text on the screen may be well justified in some situations (e.g., occasionally at an academic conference), any distractions may result in a failure here. It is the speaker's public speaking skills that are targeted here.

3. The two video clips of "Secure Yourself Online" and "The Hidden World of Chili Peppers" mentioned in Material/Preparation C are highly recommended. The instructor may ask students to find the differences between the original version and the improved version. They will sure enjoy this and learn at the same time.

Delivery

UNDERSTANDING TEACHING

I am always ready to learn although I do not always like being taught.

—Winston Churchill

"That's what education should be," I said, "the art of orientation. Educators should devise the simplest and most effective methods of turning minds around. It shouldn't be the art of implanting sight in the organ, but should proceed on the understanding that the organ already has the capacity, but is improperly aligned and isn't facing the right way."

—Plato

TEACHER'S GUIDE (Q & A)

➤ **演讲表达包括哪些内容?**

- 演讲表达是演讲内容的舞台呈现过程,至少可以从两个维度描述:演讲方式以及信息表征形式。

- 从演讲方式讲,可分为照稿宣读的演讲(reading from a manuscript)、背诵演讲(reciting from memory)、半即兴演讲(speaking extemporaneously)和即兴演讲(impromptu speech)。

- 从信息表征维度,演讲主要包括语言信息以及非语言信息的呈现。

- 英语演讲中,语言信息主要通过语音进行传递,除了音量控制以外,尤其指语音各维度的运用——单音发音和各种语流现象,如重音、节奏、语调、停顿与强调等。

- 非语言信息则主要通过面部表情、视线交流、身体姿势、手势等方式传递。

- 演讲表达常涉及如何克服怯场的话题。

➤ **该教学环节何时进行?**

- 在《演讲的艺术》第十版(中国版)教材中,该环节集中安排在:
  A. Delivering Your Speech (*APS*, Chapter 3, pp. 36–38);
  B. Delivering the Speech (*APS*, Chapter 11, pp. 146–158);
  C. Preparation and Presentation (*APS*, Chapter 16, pp. 244–245)。

- 这一教学环节可在 *APS* 教材第十一章中集中讲解,但在此之前,需要在学生的演讲实践中零星涉及。遇到一处讲解一处。

➤ 该教学环节有何必要性？

- 演讲所有的准备工作均为了舞台上的几分钟或几十分钟，演讲表达是演讲的最终体现形式。
- 在许多师生眼中，英语演讲几乎等同于演讲表达，可见其重要性。

➤ 该环节的主要教学目标是什么？

- 帮助学生了解演讲表达与内容、组织、语言之间的关系，认识演讲表达的最终目的是实现信息与情感的递送。
- 帮助学生了解演讲表达的几种方式及其使用场合。
- 帮助学生了解演讲表达中的语言及非语言信息的传递载体及实现方式。
- 帮助学生提高演讲表达技巧，尤其是声音运用和视线交流的原则和技巧，以及英语语音中的停顿、语速把握以及强调方式。

➤ 演讲表达究竟有什么技巧？

- 所有技巧都归结为两点：让听众听清楚、听明白；让听众感兴趣。
- 公众演讲是交流艺术。某种程度上，没有视线交流，便没有交流。
- 自然的表情、手势以及说话的语气与神态应促进信息的传递。
- 要让听众听明白，段落间的过渡不可少，关键信息需要多次强调。

➤ 常见的教学困难

- 大部分学生缺乏公众演讲经验，尤其是交流中的声音运用和手势、眼神等方面的处理。
- 学生英语口语能力仍有待提高，不少学生还达不到用英语流利地表述思想的程度。英语演讲的要求更高，更难以达到。
- 来自外语和公众演讲的双重焦虑，增加了学生怯场的概率。

➤ 教与学的误区

- 演讲能力主要是指即兴演讲能力。如果准备工作做得过多，就不能说明演讲能力强了。
- 演讲家大部分是天生的。
- 英语说得越快越流利，也就越好。
- 演讲就是舞台表演，所以表演很重要。

Goal:	To help students understand how ineffective delivery can negatively impact the message they are trying to convey.
Class Size:	Any.
Time:	20–40 mins.
Pre-Class Reading Assignment:	None; or Delivering the Speech (*APS*, Chapter 11, pp. 146–158).
Materials/Preparation:	Sample "Delivery Cards."

Sample "Delivery Cards"

- Style: Speak too slowly.
  Topic: Give an instruction to students (or on any other topics).

- Style: Speak too quickly.
  Topic: Explain how to register for classes at your university.

- Style: Use unnatural, overdone hand gestures.
  Topic: Discuss the importance of behaving properly at a formal graduation ceremony when the national anthem is played.

- Style: Avoid eye contact with the audience.
  Topic: Discuss the importance of making friends.

- Style: Avoid eye contact with the audience.
  Topic: Discuss the importance of equal rights for women in the workplace.

- Style: Speak too slowly.
  Topic: Tell the audience about an exciting moment in sports history (or from your own experience).

- Style: Don't use any pause.
  Topic: Explain an unfamiliar, complicated technical, mathematical, or scientific theory.

- Style: Fidget with the card while speaking.
  Topic: Give tips on how to stay calm before an exam.

- Style: Use too many pauses.
  Topic: Tell us about a scene from your favorite action movie.

- Style: Speak in a monotone.
  Topic: Tell us about the excitement involved in driving (or doing other things).

PPT/Directions	活动过程描述
1. **Break the rules!** Who's the worst speaker and best actor/actress?	1. 这个活动主要是要学生当演员，表演出各种不恰当的演讲表达方式，以让其他学生有感性认识，并深刻记忆。活动的核心在于轻松的环境、幽默的气氛，因此活动开始时气氛营造非常重要。 活动以比赛的形式进行。教师可预设一些小奖励。
2. **Volunteers** ↓ Topic card { Style / Topic } ↓ Don't disclose the required style! ↓ Preparation: Up to two minutes. Delivery: Up to one minute.	2. 向学生解释比赛规则。 A. 需要几位自愿者参与。自愿者的主要任务是展示"最差演讲风格"，活动最后将评选最佳表演。 B. 表演者会拿到一张卡片，卡片上有两条信息：一条是演讲风格特点，一条是所建议的题目。参与者将以此题目（也可以自己定题目）进行演讲，并尽力展现所要求的演讲风格。 C. 表演者不得向其他人公布卡片内容。等表演结束后，请大家猜测所要求的演讲风格。 D. 表演者有两分钟的准备时间，演讲时间不得超过一分钟。演讲主要目的是展示演讲风格。 所提供卡片中的项目可以选择使用，也可增加其他项目（参见 Materials/Preparation）。
3. Make a guess! Who's the best actor?	3. 听众事先不知道自愿者需要表演的演讲风格类型。观看演讲，然后猜测所要求的风格。如果大部分人能猜中，则说明表演者的演技高。 听众所用时间越短，则说明表演得越好。
4. Delivery matters!	4. 与学生一起总结演讲中应避免的细节问题。这时，学生应该有一个较为清晰的感受。

Comments/Reflections

1. This activity, which stresses delivery skills, can be used in a variety of instructional situations. Wherever it is used, the key to utilizing it successfully lies in providing a comfortable and constructive atmosphere for the participants.

2. Instructors often find it difficult to cover the basic elements of speech delivery, particularly when there is little time allocated in the curriculum to do so. When they do find time to discuss this,

they realize it is useless to give a lecture on it or list a series of "prescription" on board. This activity is intended to let students understand what an appropriate mode of delivery is to different speech topics by showing (not telling) them what a worst delivery style may be. More interestingly, students are actors and actresses themselves who purposefully break rules of delivery and live out their "worst case scenarios," which creates quite a relaxed and constructive environment.

3. It is encouraged that the activity is conducted early in the chapter of delivery so as to break the tension of public speaking for students.

4. When foreign language anxiety arises here, which may be predicted in many classrooms, the instructor may even allow volunteers to speak in Chinese in order to produce expected dramatic effect. Meanwhile, it is important to make students understand that good English public speaking is possible for everybody as long as full preparation is made.

5. Sample delivery card ideas provided here can be adapted to fit the topic area students may cover in their future assignments.

本活动的设计基于以下文献来源：Hayward, Pamela. (1998). Delivery Cards. In Lucas, Stephen E. (ed.) *Selections from the Speech Communication Teacher, 1994–1996*. Madison, Wisconsin: McGraw-Hill. 14–15.

16.2 Weekly Hints for Speech Delivery

Goal: To provide students with information about delivering speeches on a weekly basis.

Class Size: 25–40 students.

Time: No more than five minutes per week.

Pre-Class Reading Assignment: Delivering the Speech (*APS*, Chapter 11, pp. 146–158).

Materials/Preparation: A list of key issues in effective English speech delivery.

Key Issues in Effective English Speech Delivery

Week 2	Volume
Week 3	Rate
Week 4	Eye Contact
Week 5	Facial Expression and Posture
Week 6	Gestures and Movement
Week 7	Pause
Week 8	Personal Appearance
Week 9	English Pronunciation

In-Class Procedure

PPT/Directions	活动过程描述
Pre-Class Assignment	**课前任务（学期任务）**
1–3 Receive your assignment! ↓ Research ↓ Writing ↓ Presentation	1. 这个活动采用学期任务、周周检查、周周实践、积少成多的方式。在开学初，将八项任务（参见 Materials/Preparation）均匀地分配给全班学生，每周完成一项任务。 2. 学生需对话题展开研究，不仅需要阅读课本的第十一章，还需要查阅其他资料，包括演讲理论与实践，以及演讲点评方面的文献或视频。研究成果需形成文字稿提交。需认真准备课上的发言。 3. 第二次课上，组员合作完成以"演讲表达注意事项"为题的口头陈述，时间不超过两分钟。需清楚地陈述注意事项，必要时举例说明。

（待续）

PPT/Directions	活动过程描述
In-Class Procedure	**课堂活动过程**
4–6 Be teachers. Be judges.	4. 上课开始，第一小组先进行有关演讲技巧的微型讲座（两三分钟），之后进入其他教学环节。 5. 课上如遇演讲实践，学生进行分析时需将焦点放在学生微型讲座谈论的演讲技巧上。 6. 负责该话题的任务小组成员则成为这一方面的"权威"，在大家意见不统一时，有"最后的发言权"。 （两分钟。）
Follow-Up Procedure	**后续环节**
7. A little progress every day!	7. 连续八周，每次上课第一项活动便是学生进行的演讲表达技巧微型讲座。但每次讨论和点评环节中，应将之前做过的所有要点考虑在内。 这样，学生每周的积累就多一点儿，直到完全了解。

Comments/Reflections

1. This activity is designed to arouse students' interest in improving their speaking skills every time they enter the classroom—not just on their own speech day. Although they learn only a fraction about delivery each time, they bear in mind the whole issue of delivery all the time.

2. It is important to make sure that students do research before class and prepare a presentation based on their research.

3. It would be interesting for students to make their own checklist for delivery based on their research and presentations.

4. Encourage students to continue their exploration into the assigned topic even after their presentation and extend the research. Students would feel excited and their confidence will be enhanced when they become the arbitrator in case of disagreement.

本活动的设计基于以下文献来源：Lattin, Bohn D. (2001). Helpful Hints for Public Speaking. In Lucas, Stephen E. (ed.) *Selections from the Speech Communication Teacher, 1996–1999*. Madison, Wisconsin: McGraw-Hill. 22.

16.3　Eye Contact Shooting Gallery

Goal:	To provide students with an opportunity to develop eye contact skills for public speaking.
Class Size:	25–40 students.
Time:	10–15 mins.
Pre-Class Reading Assignment:	None; or Eye Contact (*APS*, Chapter 11, p. 154).
Materials/Preparation:	None.

🕐 In-Class Procedure

PPT/Directions	活动过程描述
1–3 *Directions:* You are going to make a very short speech of about 30 seconds on one of the most familiar topics. You have three minutes to prepare this. And you can take notes if you want. Make sure you are fully prepared because you are expected to make eye contact with every audience for at least five seconds.	1. 这是一个很简单的课堂活动，培养演讲者与听众进行视线交流的意识和技巧。活动共分为两部分：演讲准备和演讲。 2. 演讲准备。给全班学生三分钟的时间，准备一场30秒钟的即兴演讲。题目可以选择最简单、人人都有话说的，例如Who Am I?、My Favorite Subject、My Best Friend、My Hobbies等。学生也可以自选题目。可以记笔记。希望大家进行充分准备，以避免出现无话可说的情况。 3. 班上每位学生将依次上台演讲，但这次演讲的目的是要检查演讲者能否保持与听众的视线交流。

4.
 	
"I won't lower my hand until I count five."
 	
"Look at me!"
 	
"You looked away!"
 	
"You were looking over my head."
	4. 演讲。
	
	  A. 演讲者站上台后，所有学生举起手来，手心向前。
	
	  B. 演讲者演讲时，与每个学生视线交流的累计时间需要达到五秒钟。听众在感觉到演讲者的视线时，开始数数，等数到五，便可以将手放下来。
	
	  C. 当演讲结束时，看看还有多少学生举着手。听众可以给演讲者各种提醒（如左侧幻灯片所示）。
	
	班级人数少于25人时，每位学生都需上台。班级人数多时（如40人左右），可分散到两节课进行。第二节课学生的经验可能更丰富。

1. This activity was initially created for corporate executives in communication training sessions. It addresses the undesirable and often uncomfortable necessity for making eye contact with an audience, and it provides immediate feedback to students about their ability to maintain eye contact.

2. Of all the things that matter to the delivery, volume and eye contact perhaps top the list. However, beginning level learners tend to look anywhere but at their audience. Lack of eye contact would hinder a student's ability to persuade an audience as eye contact, both in the Chinese culture and the English culture, can denote sincerity, trustworthiness, and competence. Therefore, eye contact training proves to be mandatory in a speech class.

3. What is interesting about the activity is that students in the audience usually raise their hands reluctantly as the exercise begins, but show a great deal of enthusiasm by the end of the exercise.

4. When some speakers struggle to engage the audience nonverbally, the instructor may let them sit down and announce that there will be one more exercise for them later in the semester.

本活动的设计来源于以下文献: Roach, Thomas J. & Lisa J. Goodnight. (2001). Eye Contact Shooting Gallery. In Lucas, Stephen E. (ed.) *Selections from the Speech Communication Teacher, 1996–1999*. Madison, Wisconsin: McGraw-Hill. 23.

16.4 What Can We Do About the Nonverbal Area in Public Speaking?

Goal:	To arouse students' awareness of the function of nonverbal communication through sensing its impact in authentic public speaking situations, and therefore learn to make conscious use of it.
Class Size:	Less than 40 students.
Time:	40 mins.
Pre-Class Reading Assignment:	The Speaker's Voice, The Speaker's Body (*APS*, Chapter 11, pp. 150–155); The Speaker (*APS*, Chapter 12, pp. 164–165).
Materials/Preparation:	A. Pictures and video clips about two well-known public speakers (available on heep. unipus. cn). B. Video clips of students' presentations (e.g., collections of samples speeches from previous teaching years). C. Pictures and videos about Nick Vujicic, a speaker without arms and legs (available on heep. unipus. cn). D. Pictures which demonstrate nonverbal communication manners of various kinds (e.g., gestures, facial expressions...).

🕐 In-Class Procedure

PPT/Directions	活动过程描述
1–2 Nonverbal Communication How much do you know?	1. 本活动旨在让学生了解体态语言在公众演讲和交际中的作用，并学习使用。学习重点为手势和声音的运用。 2. 引入主题。教师通过体态语，如眼神、手势（例如，手指放在嘴边的姿势表示安静）作为课堂开场，让学生明白，语言之外也有信息的交流。然后，教师引入当天的主题。 （两分钟。）

（待续）

PPT/Directions	活动过程描述
3. Pictures and Videos ↓ • Who? • What in common? • What effect? ↓ Gestures Wordless: More Than Words	3. 学习手势。 全班讨论。让学生观看具体的各类演讲者的演讲手势，启发他们发现演讲中的手势语。 A. 教师以竖起大拇指这个手势为例，先让学生表述他们所知道的该手势的含义，描述在什么样的演讲中看到过这个手势。也可进而讨论手势在不同文化中的不同含义。 B. 逐一展示图片或播放视频（可参见 Materials/Preparation A, D，展示图片，录像可以只播放10–20秒钟）。 C. 让学生回答两个问题：第一，图中或视频中的人物在做什么？第二，他们有何共同之处？第三，他们的体态语言起到了什么作用？ 以自愿回答和点名回答相结合的方式来一起探讨问题。 引导学生讨论手势等非言语行为的交际作用。 （10分钟。）
4. Power of Voice and Eyes Nick Vujicic	4. 感受声音和语调对演讲内容的强化作用。 让学生观看演讲者 Nick Vujicic 的视频节选（参见 Materials/Preparation C），让学生感受演讲人的声音和眼神等体态语传递出来的信息，并讨论眼神和表情与演讲内容相结合的重要性。 A. 这位无手无脚的演讲者为什么打动了你？ B. 为什么会感动如此多的人？ （10分钟。）
5. Empower yourself with the speechless!	5. 小组实践活动。 A. 每个小组对其中一位组员的一分钟即兴演讲进行点评。 B. 要求：第一，描述非言语交际表现，重点放在手势、表情和声音上；第二，讨论这些表现的交际效果。 C. 小组讨论六分钟。要求记笔记，准备随后的小组汇报。
6. Group Report (90 seconds)	6. 小组汇报。有五至六个小组的班级可以要求每组汇报90秒钟，更大的班级可采取缩短汇报时间或减少汇报小组数量的形式。教师应该给予点评。

（待续）

PPT/Directions	活动过程描述
Assignment	**课后作业**
7. Online Discussion	7. 将学生课堂演讲录像或者其他视频资料放在网上的公共平台，让学生对演讲者的手势、声音、体态等进行欣赏与评价。有条件的情况下，可以上传口头或书面点评，或在论坛上讨论。

Comments/Reflections

1. This activity is designed to help students understand the power of nonverbal communication, especially that of gestures and voice. The two focuses are reflected in Steps 4 and 5 of the in-class procedure.

2. The activity guides students to sense out the occurrence of nonverbal signs in public speaking and stimulate their curiosity to explore the area of the "speechless" communication. Consequently, it encourages students to make use of these nonverbal communication strategies.

3. Materials used for the activity may be easily found from the online sources, so the instructor may select what is appropriate to his or her own class.

4. This kind of activity works better for small classes and beginning level learners.

（供稿人：丁洁 洛阳师范学院；改编人：田朝霞）

Speeches of Specific Types

17

Introductory/"Ice-Breaker" Speeches

UNDERSTANDING TEACHING

We are each gifted in a unique and important way. It is our privilege and our adventure to discover our own special light.

—*Mary Dunbar*

Explore your mind, discover yourself, then give the best that is in you to your age and to your world. There are heroic possibilities waiting to be discovered in every person.

—*Wilfred Peterson*

TEACHER'S GUIDE (Q & A)

➤ **自我介绍演讲与自我介绍不同吗？**

- 大家都熟悉"自我介绍"，每个人在不同场合也实践过。但自我介绍演讲和我们熟悉的"自我介绍"的确不同。它们之间的差异也集中体现了演讲和日常口语会话的不同。

- 对比两者，自我介绍演讲具有以下几个特点：第一，在较为正式的场合进行，演讲结构必须完整，应包括开头、主体和结尾三个部分；第二，演讲所传递的思想较为复杂，但有突出的中心和明确的观点；第三，对自己进行深度剖析和挖掘，描述自己的性格、文化背景、信仰、理想、价值观等。无论是一分钟演讲，还是三分钟演讲，自我介绍演讲应该体现这三个特点。自我介绍演讲不宜过长，《演讲的艺术》第十版（中国版）教材要求进行两分钟自我介绍演讲。

- 自我介绍演讲强调创造性，常要求演讲者以富有创新性和想象力的方式对自己进行介绍，因此比喻、象征等修辞手法较为常用。

➤ **自我介绍演讲与介绍致辞有何不同吗？**

- 自我介绍演讲（introductory speech）与介绍致辞（speech of introduction）的介绍对象不同，前者为自己介绍自己，后者为自己介绍别人。

- 自我介绍演讲更多地强调以艺术手法将自己不为人知的一面展示出来，而介绍致辞则是对发言嘉宾进行引见。

- 介绍致辞可能不需要像自我介绍演讲那样有完整、复杂的结构。其特点详见 Unit 20 Speeches for Special Occasions。

➤ 该教学环节何时进行?

- 在《演讲的艺术》第十版（中国版）教材中，该环节集中安排在第三章"你的第一次演讲"（Giving Your First Speech, *APS*, Chapter 3, pp. 32–43）。教师完成演讲前两章演讲概述之后，以此进入演讲知识的系统学习。

➤ 该教学环节何必要性?

- 这一环节是学生的第一次演讲尝试，也常称为"破冰"环节（ice-breaker）。学生开始从以前在英语课上或英语角所进行的"自我介绍"过渡到正式的演讲。除安排学生进行自我介绍演讲外，也可安排学生介绍同班同学。
- 这一环节担任着几重任务：第一，让学生从最熟悉的话题开始，舒缓焦虑，激发兴趣；第二，以最熟悉的话题入手，让学生了解演讲与日常会话的差别，了解演讲的基本特点。

➤ 常见的教学困难

- 第一大困难是因为外语和公众演讲的双重焦虑，学生不能开口。需要教师充分理解学生的状况。一方面，尽量降低外语焦虑，如引导学生进行必要的准备，包括写演讲稿，让学生选择自己最感兴趣、最熟悉的方面来讲；另一方面，教师应尽可能活跃气氛。必要时，教师可以考虑适当降低要求，以鼓励学生乐于开口为主要关注点。
- 学生不能区分演讲和平时的自我介绍之间的区别。自我介绍演讲在内容深度、组织结构以及语言运用上都高于日常会话场合的自我介绍。教师可借助学生教材中的两个典型例子来分析自我介绍演讲的几个特点（参见第一个问题），特别是其创造性（creativity）：

  1) "Pot, Soil, Water" (*APS*, p. 39);
  2) "Confronting Myself: Color in the Wind" (*APS*, p. 41).

➤ 教与学的误区

- 自我介绍演讲就是一般的自我介绍，就是介绍我的姓名、家庭、职业、爱好等。
- 自我介绍演讲不需要准备。
- 自我介绍演讲就是信息性演讲，告知信息。
- 自我介绍演讲和介绍致辞是一回事。

17.1 Self-Introduction

Goal:	To learn to introduce oneself in an impressive way.
Class Size:	Any.
Time:	10 mins.
Pre-Class Reading Assignment:	Giving Your First Speech (*APS*, Chapter 3, pp. 32–43).
Materials/Preparation:	None.

In-Class Procedure

PPT/Directions	活动过程描述
1–2 Guess which statement is false about me: • I have been teaching English for more than 10 years! • I once won the first prize in Hubei Provincial English Speaking Contest. • I have a lovely daughter who is five years old now. • I traveled to many places such as Shanghai, Beijing, Guilin and so on!	1. 教师展示四个与自己相关的句子（此处为示范，教师可更换描述），请学生猜测哪个句子与自己信息不符，并说明理由。只需要选择一两位学生即可，每位学生的时间为45秒至一分钟。 2. 教师公布答案，并根据信息正确的三个句子进行简短的自我介绍。时间为一分钟。
3. Statements • Impressive • Ambiguous • Creative	3. 教师讲解这四个句子的选择标准，四个句子的选择既要有典型性、创造性又要有迷惑性，加大猜测的难度。然后向学生展示最开始关于描写自己的四句话，结合标准予以点评。
4–5 • He is a very influential person in Chinese sport field. • He has won a lot of honors for his country as well as himself. • He got injured in a match. • He is good at hurdle race.	4. 请学生判断如左侧幻灯片所示的这四句话是否符合以上三个原则。 5. 如果符合，能否猜出这四句话描写的是谁？（答案：刘翔。）

（待续）

PPT/Directions	活动过程描述
6–8 **Introduce Yourself** Write four statements about yourself, one of which is false. Report these statements to your group and ask them to guess which is false and why. Then each group selects one to report his or her statements to the class and let all guess.	6. 教师讲解完后，让学生参与。首先将全班分成若干小组，每组四至五人。 7. 小组每位成员写出四个与自己信息相关的句子（其中有一个句子不符合自己的情况），然后请其他组员猜测。之后根据符合自己的三句话进行简短自我介绍。 8. 每个小组选出一位学生到讲台上进行刚才的活动。
	9. 教师就每位上台的学生提供的四句话以及简短的自我介绍进行点评。

Comments/Reflections

1. This activity is designed for the following considerations. First, it creates a warm and friendly learning atmosphere. Second, it arouses students' curiosity to learn more. Third, it improves students' creativity. Fourth, it makes students understand a special way to introduce oneself.

2. This activity is also a very good warm-up activity to engage students in classroom learning.

3. When preparing this activity, the instructor must bear one rule in mind, that is, to choose the words which are very general, creative and deceptive; otherwise some students will know the answer when they see the first word in the PPT. So it is very crucial to choose the right words and examples to maintain the suspense and interest of this activity. However, the examples cannot be some extreme cases. They must be the persons most people know.

（供稿人：陆小丽 湖北大学；改编人：周红兵）

17.2

Who Am I?—Describing a Person

Goal:	To create an entertaining environment for students to practice making an introductory speech.
Class Size:	Any.
Time:	10–30 mins.
Pre-Class Reading Assignment:	Giving Your First Speech (*APS*, Chapter 3, pp. 32–43); Using Language (*APS*, Chapter 10, pp. 130–144).
Materials/Preparation:	None.

🕐 In-Class Procedure

PPT/Directions	活动过程描述
1–2 *Directions:* We need a volunteer—a speaker to come to the front and make a guess about the identity of a person. This person's information will be given later. Everybody will know who that person is except the volunteer. But the volunteer may ask the audience up to 10 questions, to which the answer can only be "Yes" or "No," and try to find out the answer.	1. 告诉学生游戏规则：一位自愿者站到台前，根据所提供的信息，猜测一个人的身份。自愿者可以向听众最多提10个问题，听众只能回答"是"或"不是"。 2. 邀请自愿者上台，提醒自愿者问问题时要动脑筋，以最有效地利用10次机会。每个问题之间的间隔时间不能超过10秒。也就是问完第一个问题后，10秒钟之内必须问第二个问题。
3. Game time. > • I am an American, a male in the 50s. > • To some extent, I am the most powerful man in the US. > • I am a graduate of Columbia University and Harvard Law School. > • I care for the well-being of all American citizens. > • Who am I?	3. 热身游戏。选取两位自愿者，自愿者面对听众，背对显示信息的PPT。自愿者需要猜出教师介绍的是谁。先猜出答案者为胜者。 4. PPT显示奥巴马的照片，教师提醒听众保密。 5. 有关奥巴马的四条信息以动画形式逐条播放，教师则跟随动画朗读该条信息。 6. 自愿者从听到第一条信息起即可抢答，但也可以选择听完几条后再抢答。 7. 对于先猜出正确答案的自愿者，请他（她）先进行一个口头的人物描述——40秒钟简短的介绍性演讲，然后解密描述对象的身份。对出色完成任务的同学进行奖励或鼓励。此时，另外一位自愿者将进入下一个游戏，以示处罚。 8. 若自愿者未能完成任务，则邀请一位听众上台完成40秒钟的人物介绍。同时该自愿者将进入下一个游戏，以示处罚。

（待续）

PPT/Directions	活动过程描述
9 **Who is she?** • She, born on 12 July 1997, is a Pakistani activist for female education and the youngest-ever Nobel Laureate. • She is known mainly for human rights advocacy for education and for women in her country.	9. 换一个人物，重复该游戏，重复次数可依据具体情境需要。左边PPT所示马拉拉为第二例。找出第二位玩下一轮游戏的自愿者（因为前面已经找出一位）。
10–11 1. Li Na (李娜) 2. Jay Chou (周杰伦) 3. Zhao Wei (赵薇)	10. 第三轮游戏，可选择多位人物。人物选择一般为热点人物，也可根据本班同学兴趣决定。 自愿者面对听众，可以向听众提最多10个问题，每个问题都是可能与PPT上的人物相关，问题必须是一般疑问句，听众只能回答"是"或"不是"。 11. 最后自愿者把自己问的10条内容信息归纳出来，改成一篇一分钟左右的介绍性演讲，同时也要说出自己描述的人物的姓名。（此游戏有一定的难度，教师可以选择课堂上比较活跃、性格外向的学生，同时第一个人物的设置不要太难。）

Comments/Reflections

1. This activity is designed for the following considerations. First, it creates a light and entertaining learning atmosphere. Second, it provides a good example of how to capture the hallmarks of a person, which is important to an introductory speech. Third, it stimulates students to think as well when they have to get the answer by asking fewer questions.

2. The activity applies to both small classes and big ones.

3. The activity works better for beginning level learners who are less able to produce longer speeches on their own. Intermediate and advanced level students should be encouraged to produce more complicated language output with the help of prompts.

4. An extended activity or an alternative might be like this: One group (or the representative) from the audience gives an introductory speech about a person everyone in the classroom is familiar with. Other groups ask questions to find out the real identity of the person described.

5. A brief form of the activity (e.g., to guess only one person) may serve as a warm-up activity at the beginning of a lesson just to arouse students' interest.

18

Informative Speeches

UNDERSTANDING TEACHING

The enemy of learning is knowing.

—*Steve Ahn*

Those who expect to reap the blessings of freedom must undergo the fatigue of supporting it.

—*T. Paine*

TEACHER'S GUIDE (Q & A)

➤ **信息性演讲有哪些类型?**

信息性演讲并不是简单地介绍事情，它可以分为以下四种:
- 关于实物的信息性演讲。
- 关于过程的信息性演讲。
- 关于事件的信息性演讲。
- 关于概念的信息性演讲。

➤ **如何判断信息性演讲的成败?**

- 信息传达是否准确。
- 信息传达是否清晰。
- 信息传达是否让听众感到有趣且有意义。

➤ **该教学环节何时进行?**

- 在《演讲的艺术》第十版（中国版）教材中，该环节集中安排在第十三章"信息性演讲"（Speaking to Inform, *APS*, Chapter 13, pp. 176–191）。学习本单元之前，学生需对公众演讲的要素（第一、二章）、你的第一次演讲（第三章）、语言的运用（第十章）、演讲表达（第十一章）等章节内容有基本的了解。

➤ 信息性演讲应主要注意哪些方面的问题?

- 信息性演讲在实施的过程中，演讲者一般会借助一些视觉辅助。但是视觉辅助的方式一定要因情况因形势而定。适当的视觉辅助会使演讲锦上添花，而不合适的视觉辅助则会使演讲效果适得其反。
- 信息性演讲者要遵守的基本演讲准则:
  - 不要高估听众的知识水平。
  - 不要过于专业化。
  - 使观点个性化。
  - 避免抽象表达。
  - 要有创意。

➤ 常见的教学困难

- 学生有时过分依赖视觉辅助，尤其是PPT，经常是学生对着PPT进行演讲，缺乏掌控视觉辅助设施的基本技能，从而忽略了听众，也没有办法根据听众的反馈来适时调整自己的演讲。
- 学生在实际进行信息性演讲的过程中，经常出现的问题是时间控制问题。很多学生无法在规定的时间内完成自己的演讲任务。学生在演讲材料与演讲表达方面还要进一步的练习与提高。
- 很多学生在进行信息性演讲时，会涉及很多与自己本专业相关的知识，有时会让不是本专业的听众理解起来较为困难。如何处理自己的演讲语言，或者说如何使自己的语言变得通俗易懂，也是信息性演讲比较难操作的一个方面。

➤ 教与学的误区

- 在视觉辅助的选择与使用上，学生认为只要提供必要的视觉辅助，演讲就一定会表达得更清楚。
- 忽视了听众分析，经常把自己的主观想法强加到听众身上，认为自己感兴趣的话题与内容，听众也一定会感兴趣。
- 认为信息性演讲主要是强调信息的准确、清晰，语言与其他技巧不是很重要，因而很少用到其他的演讲表达技巧，演讲者就只是一位信息播报员。

18.1

What Is It?—Informing Others

Goal:	To help students have a deep impression about four types of informative speeches and visual aids.
Class Size:	About 50 students.
Time:	15–20 mins.
Pre-Class Reading Assignment:	Using Visual Aids (*APS*, Chapter 12, pp. 160–175); Speaking to Inform (*APS*, Chapter 13, pp. 176–191).
Materials/Preparation:	None.

🕐 In-Class Procedure

PPT/Directions	活动过程描述
1–3 *Directions:* Brainstorm words associated with the following types. 1) Objects; 2) Concepts; 3) Events; 4) Process of making something. Try to find as many words as you can, and write them on a piece of paper.	1. 告诉学生活动规则：将邀请四位自愿者上台进行简单的30秒钟头脑风暴活动（一人负责一个类别，并且把自己所想到的单词写在黑板上），在每一类别后面写出尽可能多的单词，越多越好。 2. 给全班同学大约一分钟时间检查与学习四位自愿者的归类，如归类有误，可请其他学生纠正。 3. 教师进行点评反馈，鼓励学生，让学生更自信，因为他们都能够想出很多的相关词条。
4–6 Read the following words carefully: Taoism　　　Bird　　　Computer Amplifier　　Plane　　　Beauty Hurricane　　Bacteria　　Cell Homosexual What topics can arouse your interest? Explain why.	4. 逐条播放如左侧幻灯片所示的词条。目的：播放各种话题，以希望能够满足不同学生的兴趣，使每位学生都能够找到自己感兴趣的信息点与话题，同时还能够锻炼学生的瞬时记忆能力。 5. 给学生30秒钟完成头脑风暴和思考，并让学生选择自己觉得最新颖的话题，注意话题种类的多样性。 6. 在全班选取三位学生，叫他们说出自己觉得比较新颖的话题，并且简要说明原因。教师可以简要回顾一下以前学过的如何选择话题与演讲目的的教学内容，建议三至五分钟。

（待续）

PPT/Directions	活动过程描述
7. The definition of informative speech. The types of informative speeches.	7. 教师讲解以上的话题均可成为典型的信息性演讲话题，解释信息性演讲的定义，并介绍其四种分类。
8–9 Power of visual aids.	8. 引导学生思考如何进行好一场精彩的信息性演讲，引出视觉辅助对信息性演讲的重要性。 9. 简要说明视觉辅助使用的四点要求。
10. Types of visual aids: 1) Objects and models; 2) Photographs and drawings; 3) Graphs; 4) Charts; 5) Video; 6) The speaker; 7) Powerpoint.	10. 介绍七种视觉辅助物。尽量使用课堂中的东西作为话题或者视觉辅助，如在线扩音器、手机、笔袋、iPad等。
11 Show time!	11. 请四位自愿者从头脑风暴中的新话题中选取不同话题，各进行40秒至一分钟的信息性演讲。教师进行简要点评。

Comments/Reflections

1. This activity incorporates the use of visual aids into the study of informative speech theory. First, it makes the class more entertaining since it combines activity and theory learning. Second, it provides a good example of how to narrow down a topic for an informative speech. Third, it stimulates all students to be involved in the class activity.

2. The activity applies to medium-sized classes.

3. The activity will be more productive if intermediate and advanced level students are encouraged to produce well-organized informative speeches before class.

(供稿人：汪希平 皖西学院；改编人：周红兵)

18.2　Tell You What I Am Good at—Challenge to Inform

Goal:	To offer students an opportunity to get to know each other better in practicing how to make an informative speech.
Class Size:	Any.
Time:	30–45 mins.
Pre-Class Reading Assignment:	Speaking to Inform (*APS*, Chapter 13, pp. 176–191).
Materials/Preparation:	A video clip from movie *Larry Crowne* (28: 56–32: 00) (available on http://heep. unipus. cn).

In-Class Procedure

PPT/Directions	活动过程描述
1–2 Group members give short speeches in turn. ↓ Group discussion: 1) Is the information clear? 2) Is it interesting? 3) Did the speaker use any visual aids? 4) Did the speaker use any nonverbal communicative skills?	1. 将学生分组，以三到四人一组为宜。轮流向组员介绍自己所擅长做的一件事情。每位学生介绍的时间为两分钟。 2. 每位组员介绍完以后，其他成员可就其所讲的内容，从以下几个方面进行评价：传递的信息是否清楚、准确、有意义、有趣；是否需要视觉辅助；如果已经用了视觉辅助，视觉辅助是否恰到好处等。
3. Presentation of each group.	3. 选出组内最好的演讲者，代表本组在全班进行展示。 4. 当所有的学生代表都完成了演讲后，教师对他们的演讲进行口头点评，点评要包含正面的与负面的评价。
5. How to inform effectively? ↓ Video clip.	5. 结合问题"如何进行一场效果非同凡响的信息性演讲"，观看电影 *Larry Crowne* 的视频片断（参见Materials/Preparation，共四位演讲者）。 6. 教师提问学生如何进行一篇成功的信息性演讲。

（待续）

PPT/Directions	活动过程描述
7. Group discussion: what's the key to a successful informative speech?	7. 各小组进行第二次讨论，讨论视频中演讲者在进行信息性演讲时所存在的问题。（六分钟。）
8. Presentation of each group.	8. 各组代表轮流在全班演讲。演讲时间为每组三分钟。 9. 教师就学生演讲进行点评。

Comments/Reflections

1. The major goal of this activity is to help students acquire certain skills in delivering an informative speech. It is usually not that easy for English learners to give this type of speech with accurate and clear information and at the same time to make it meaningful and interesting to the audience. Let students choose to talk about what they are good at and familiar with. This could help them focus on applying the techniques to the final delivery.

2. Small classes are preferred, for students could make careful assessment and improvement in group presentation.

3. Students can be divided into groups of three or four. For beginners, a list of suggested topics, such as how to purchase on the Internet, how to write a love letter, how to deal with an emergent fire alarm, could be given in advance. Each group picks one topic from the list, and all group members prepare their own version before class. After group presentation, four versions should be fully analyzed to figure out both the strong and weak points, and thus to make a better version for the representative to deliver later in class.

4. Students of intermediate and advanced level are free to choose their topics. The idea is that, the more familiar they are, the better output would be produced.

5. A brief form of the activity (e.g., only two or three speakers prepare beforehand and deliver the speech in class) may serve as the lead-in activity at the beginning of a lesson focusing on how to give an informative speech about process.

（供稿人：肖琪 文华学院；改编人：周红兵）

Persuasive Speeches

UNDERSTANDING TEACHING

I taught you everything you know. But I didn't teach you everything I know.

—*Orson Scott Card*

Instructors have three loves: love of learning, love of learners, and the love of bringing the first two loves together.

—*Scott Hayden*

Truth persuades by teaching, but does not teach by persuading.

—*Tertullian*

TEACHER'S GUIDE (Q & A)

➤ **说服性演讲与信息性演讲之间的主要区别在哪里?**

- 从交流的主要目的出发，可将演讲分为至少两大类：说服性演讲和信息性演讲。信息性演讲主要目的在于信息递送本身，即让听众"知道"或"了解"；而说服性演讲的目的在于"改变"听众的思想或行为。

- 说服性演讲在提供理由、证明观点时，必然会包含信息递送，但说服性演讲中包含的信息递送，其主要目的是为了论证或说服。

➤ **该教学环节何时进行?**

- 在《演讲的艺术》第十版（中国版）教材中，该环节集中安排在第十四章"说服性演讲"（Speaking to Persuade, *APS*, Chapter 14, pp. 192–221）。学习本单元之前，学生需对公众演讲的要素（第一章）及一般过程（第四至十一章）有基本了解。

- 说服性演讲可以放在信息性演讲之后学习，也可与信息性演讲进行比对，同时进行。这种情况下，学生应该已对英语说明文和议论文的修辞特点有所了解。

➤ **该教学环节有何必要性?**

- 说服性演讲是公众演讲的最高境界，几乎所有经典演讲都是说服性的。

- 说服性演讲作为公众交流艺术，其中包含的三种基本诉求方式，即理性诉求（logos）、伦理诉求（ethos）和情感诉求（pathos），均为大学生应了解的基本知识。

- 关于说服与辩论的艺术，学生已有各种经验，尤其是在汉语、英语作文学习中接触过，但知识体系均不够系统。

➤ 说服性演讲的主要内容包括哪些？

- 帮助学生区分说服性演讲与信息性演讲。
- 帮助学生系统了解和掌握说服性演讲的主要类型及其不同的组织形式：
  - 基于事实的论题（on questions of fact）；
  - 基于价值观的论题（on questions of value）；
  - 基于政策的论题（on questions of policy）。
- 帮助学生理解亚里士多德提出的论辩三要素，即理性诉求、伦理诉求和情感诉求的含义，以及与之对应的四种常用说服方法：建立可信度（building credibility）、使用论据（using evidence）、论证（reasoning）、利用情感诉求（appealing to emotions）。
- 帮助学生系统了解和掌握基本的论证方法：归纳论证（reasoning from specific instances）、演绎论证（reasoning from principle）、因果论证（causal reasoning）、类比论证（analogical reasoning）。
- 培养学生辨别逻辑谬论的能力。常见的逻辑谬误包括：
  - 错误归因（false cause）；
  - 草率作结（hasty generalization or overgeneralization）；
  - 无效类比（invalid analogy）；
  - 转移话题（red herring）；
  - 人身攻击（ad hominem）；
  - 从众效应（bandwagon or appeal to popularity）；
  - 滑坡谬误（slippery slope）。

➤ 常见的教学困难

- 学生有时不能区分说服性演讲和信息性演讲。
- 学生有时表现浮躁，不能静下心将一个论点研究清楚，讲透彻，导致演讲总是浮于表面，不能深入。
- 绝大部分学生并未系统学习有关诉求方式、论证方法以及逻辑谬误方面的知识；同时，又未意识到这些内容的重要性。

➤ 教与学的误区

- 说服性演讲谁都会，不需要学习；只需要学一学演讲表达就行了。
- 要成功地说服听众，演讲者一定要煽情，最好能让听众掉眼泪，其他的都不重要。
- 演讲是否成功，关键看辩论是否成功。
- 成功的演讲者一定是雄辩家，一定要在气势上压倒别人。
- 学习说服性演讲就是学习雄辩；学习雄辩就要学习诡辩，要善于学习巧妙地运用逻辑谬误和攻击逻辑谬误。
- 演讲准备过程中不需要大量查阅资料，主要靠观点新奇或视角独特取胜。

19.1 Organization for Policy Speeches: Problem-Solution Order

Goal:	To help students understand the problem-solution organizational pattern for policy speeches through practice.
Class Size:	Any.
Time:	20–30 mins.
Pre-Class Reading Assignment:	Organizing Speeches on Questions of Policy (*APS*, Chapter 14, pp. 200–204).
Materials/Preparation:	Three topic cards.

Topic Card 1

- We really need to conserve natural resources.
- We must help children cure their Internet addiction.
- We must foster harmonious relationship with our roommates.

Topic Card 2

- We should prepare for our future career now.
- We must improve the traffic situation in big cities now.
- Universities should encourage general education.

Topic Card 3

- Each individual should do their part in the environmental protection.
- Higher education should prioritize creativity.
- The government must address the needs of aging population.

In-Class Procedure

PPT/Directions	活动过程描述
1–2 Activity Outline Sample Analysis ↓ Practice	1. 向学生说明本活动的目的，即掌握关于政策的说服性演讲的一种常用组织方法：问题—出路顺序。 2. 首先，教师给学生展示问题—出路顺序所适合的演讲类型范例（五分钟左右）； 然后，让学生进行实践，巩固并拓展。包括两个环节：小组讨论（约八分钟）及汇报与点评（每组不超过三分钟）。
3. Topic: We Should Strike a Proper Balance Between Work and Health.	3. 通过PPT向学生提供一个关于政策的说服性演讲话题，如左侧幻灯片所示。这一环节为演讲案例分析。 4. 分析之前，可提问一两位学生，如这个演讲应如何进行组织？即兴作答，以活跃气氛，激发思考。

5.
 	
Specific purpose: To persuade my audience that we should strike a proper balance between work and health.
 	
Central idea: Heavy workload and excessive working hours which jeopardize people's health in today's world call our attention and urge us to make a change.
 	
Main points:
I. Heavy workload and excessive working hours, which derive from or lead to stress and anxiety, are severely undermining people's health.
II. To address the problem, we must take care of work and health at the same time.
  A. Prioritizing job tasks may effectively relieve workload and accordingly relieve stress.
  B. Physical exercise is absolutely necessary for all stressed white-collar workers.
	5. 教师开始分析该问题—出路顺序组织方法样例，需以提纲形式展示演讲目的、核心观点以及分论点等部分。如左侧幻灯片所示。这一案例也为下面紧接着的学生活动提供范例。
	
	演讲目的：……
	
	核心观点：……
	
	分论点一
	    理由或解释一
	    理由或解释二
	
	分论点二
	    理由或解释一
	    理由或解释二
	  ……

（待续）

PPT/Directions	活动过程描述
6. Specific purpose: (To persuade that a policy should be taken.) Central idea: (Why? And what to do?) Main points: I. Problem II. Solution 　A. …	6. 讲解时，需特别强调几个部分的逻辑关系。在范例分析完毕之后，需将逻辑关系图示（如左侧幻灯片所示）给学生，以加深印象。 7. 范例展示完毕，组织学生以小组为单位，进行实践，巩固所学知识。 8. 将事先准备好的演讲话题卡（参见Materials/Preparation）分发给各小组，一个小组领取一张。可按照小组数量复印三张卡片。小组拿到的卡片可以相同，也可以不同。一张卡片的话题数量最好不超过三个，以尽量减少阅读题目所占用的课堂时间，而将重点放在内容的组织方法上。 9. 话题卡仅为一时想不到话题的学生提供提示，故各小组既可从卡片中挑选一个话题进行讨论，也可自定选题。
10. Specific purpose: (To persuade that a policy should be taken.) _____ Central idea: (Why? And what to do?) _____ Main points: I. Problem _____ II. Solution 　A. _____ 　B. _____	10. 要求学生在一分钟之内定题，然后讨论该话题的具体组织方式。小组讨论在六分钟之内完成，需完成笔记，笔记框架如左侧幻灯片所示。笔记将作为小组讨论之后的一分半钟口头汇报的提纲。最后再留一分钟进行演讲表达准备。 11. 讨论完毕，邀请各组代表上讲台进行汇报。 学生的常见问题为演讲内容逻辑松散（通俗地讲，即演讲目的、核心观点及分论点不能相互照应），故需提示听众学生在听报告时，审视以下几点： A. Does the central idea respond to the specific purpose? B. Do the main points effectively elaborate the central idea? C. Is the solution feasible?
	12. 每一场小组汇报结束后，教师可采用点评或班级讨论的方式对口头汇报进行回应。

Comments/Reflections

1. The vital goal of this activity is to learn this specific organizational pattern—the problem-solution order—for policy speeches (although other aspects of a speech are inevitably involved); therefore, the instructor must watch closely whether students are consciously or unconsciously using this method.

2. A likely problem may be that students tend to pay too much attention to a detail, e.g., one of the symptoms of the problems or one of the solutions, yet fail to present the overall structure of the speech. When this occurs, the instructor should remind them of the coherence between the specific purpose, the central idea and the main points.

3. Another predictable problem may be that students tend to spend a lot of time deciding about a topic. They may discuss about each of the three topics they were given in detail, which takes too much time and at the same time is not necessary. Topics are provided simply to save time as the focus of this activity is the organizational pattern. So, the instructor should make sure that students do not go astray.

4. The activity may appear in different forms to address different needs.

   A. Here is a brief version. The instructor invites only three groups to present their oral reports; however, he or she invites comments from other groups to redress any imbalance in participation. This applies to a large class too.

   B. A briefer version would be that only one topic is given to all groups for discussion, and then only one volunteer group gives an oral report. After that, the instructor organizes or facilitates class discussion, which, again focuses on the organizational pattern.

   C. Another alternative may be this. Only two steps of the activities are gone through in class—the sample analysis given by the instructor and a brief group discussion about the topics. No oral presentations. Instead, a writing assignment is given to students after class, in which case further discussion or feedback should be given next time.

5. The activity may well be extended.

   A. Extended from one organizational pattern (problem-solution order) to other patterns for policy speeches, e.g., problem-cause-solution order, comparative advantages order, motivated sequence (*ASP*, pp. 200–204);

   B. Extended from patterns for speeches on questions of policy to those for speeches on question of fact (*ASP*, p. 196) and speeches on questions of value (*ASP*, p. 198).

The extended versions are better adopted for revision and consolidation of knowledge and skills after a lecture on the persuasive speech as a whole has been given. The instructor may find these alternatives are more appealing to a large class.

The changes made to the original activity may include:

   A. The sample analysis may become a brief summary of the three types of persuasive speeches and their typical organizational patterns. Or, this step may be removed if the activity is done immediately after the lecture.

   B. The topic cards should contain topics for various types of persuasive speeches. So, change the topics for the specific purposes.

（供稿人：刘瑛 吉首大学；改编人：田朝霞）

Goal: To help students practice the problem-cause-solution order in making a persuasive speech on a given topic under the guidance of the instructor.

Class Size: Any.

Time: 20–30 mins.

Pre-Class Reading Assignment: Persuasive Speeches on Questions of Policy, Methods of Persuasion (*APS*, Chapter 14, pp. 199–216).

Materials/Preparation:
A. Materials concerning Susan Anthony's life and her speech on women's rights for suffrage.
B. Quotes about men and women.

Quotes About Men and Women

- A man's face is his autobiography. A woman's face is her work of fiction. —Oscar Wilde
- Just as women's bodies are softer than men's, so their understanding is sharper. —Christine de Pizan
- ... until opportunity is as free from sex discrimination as the right to vote finally came to be, no man has any right to criticize women for failure to measure up to men. —Mary Barnett Gilson

---

C. A list of eliciting questions.

A List of Eliciting Questions

- Do you feel good/bad for being a boy/girl? In what ways? Given a choice, would you wish to be the opposite gender? Why?
- Do you feel you are treated equally in education, employment, etc.? Illustrate your opinion.
- What's your expectation of your future marriage—the role of you and your spouse in both career development and family life? Why?
- How do you think of Susan Anthony being single all her life? Would you boys be willing to choose such a woman as a girlfriend or wife? Would you girls prefer to be such a pioneer woman at the cost of remaining single all your life?

...

D. Words and expression related to feminism.

Words and Expression Related to Feminism

sex/gender, sexism, sexist;

female, feminine, femininity;

feminist, feminism, Feminist Movement;

male, masculine, masculinity, male chauvinism, chauvinist, chauvinistic;

…

⏱ In-Class Procedure

PPT/Directions	活动过程描述
Pre-Class Assignment	**课前任务**
1. Assignment Get to know Susan Anthony.	1. 前一次课结束后，将Susan Anthony的演讲放在网上的公共平台或邮箱，要求学生认真阅读，并了解相关信息。
2–4 Lead-in Quotes about men and women. Informative Speeches • Susan Anthony • Her speech	2. 以关于男人和女人的名言（参见Materials/Preparation B）作为导入，请学生谈谈自己对名言的解读与看法。 3. 请一至两位学生陈述Susan Anthony的生平，进行一分钟的信息性演讲。 4. 再请一位同学陈述Susan Anthony演讲的主要内容：她演讲的目的是什么？为什么提出这样的观点？仍为信息性演讲，时间不超过90秒。 （10分钟。）
5. Organization of a persuasive speech (group discussion) Issue: What's wrong? ↓ Cause ↓ Solution	5. 将事先准备好的问题单（参见Materials/Preparation C）分发给小组。小组先对问题进行讨论，然后选择一个目前存在有关男女平等的现实问题进行讨论。讨论从三个方面进行： A. 现在存在什么性别歧视的问题？（提醒学生只能针对一个现象来讨论。） B. 引起这种情况的原因是什么？ C. 有什么解决方法？为什么这种方法可以奏效？ 考虑到学生的英语词汇局限，也可将相关的词汇或词汇提示展示在屏幕上供学生参考（如类似Materials/Preparation D的材料）。 （10分钟。）

（待续）

PPT/Directions	活动过程描述
6. Class Report Discussion Debate Gender equality? Gender discrimination?	6. 讨论完毕，各小组在全班进行小组口头陈述。陈述时间不超过两分钟。 A. 口头陈述的组织方式必须遵循"问题—原因—解决方式"的顺序。 B. 每一小组陈述结束后，教师可向演讲人提问，也可鼓励其他小组提问。 C. 教师可以打乱小组顺序，让观点相反的小组组成辩论擂台。如果这样做，则需要教师在小组讨论时，先了解一下各组的演讲题目。 （15—20分钟。）

Comments/Reflections

1. This activity selects a hot topic, in particular closely related to all students so that everybody may feel he or she has a lot to say. It can be safely predicted, as it has also been proven in teaching practice, that students will be very excited.

2. Heated discussion and debates about Susan Anthony and gender discrimination channel students to active critical thinking and more reflections on the role of public speaking in advancing social progress either in history or in contemporary life.

3. Both the topics of Susan Anthony's life story and Feminist Movement may be suitable for informative speeches. Therefore the instructor will find a good opportunity for students to practice speaking to inform as well.

4. The instructor should help students connect what is focused in this lesson to what has previously been learned, e.g., "Supporting Your Ideas," "Organizing the Body of the Speech," and "Beginning and Ending the Speech."

（供稿人：万玲 首都医科大学；改编人：田朝霞）

Goal:	To acquaint students with the main types of logical fallacies, so that they will be able to identify loopholes and at the same time avoid committing these fallacies.
Class Size:	Any.
Time:	30–40 mins.
Pre-Class Reading Assignment:	Methods of Persuasion (*APS*, Chapter 14, pp. 205–216).
Materials/Preparation:	A number of cards, each of which contains three examples of different logical fallacies.

Card 1

A. All my classmates are preparing for study abroad. I must sign up for a TOEFL class too this weekend.

B. Students should be allowed to look at their textbooks during examinations. After all, surgeons have X-rays to guide them during an operation; lawyers have briefs to guide them during a trial; carpenters have blueprints to guide them when they are building a house. Why, then, shouldn't students be allowed to look at their textbooks during an examination?

C. I think that we should make the academic requirements stricter for students. I recommend that you support this because we are in a budget crisis and we do not want our salaries affected.

Card 2

D. Every day I wear black shoes. One time, I was in a pair of white shoes and an accident happened to me. I've always been in black shoes ever since.

E. You can't believe the man called John Smith when he says the proposed policy would help the economy. He's just had a divorce and he doesn't even have a job. You should believe Jack; after all, he is a Christian.

F. Hugh Hefner, founder of *Playboy* magazine, has argued against censorship of pornography. But Hefner is an immature, self-indulgent millionaire... His argument, therefore, is worthless.

Card 3

G. My grandpa smoked four packs of cigarettes a day since 20 and lived until 89. Therefore, smoking really can't be that bad for you.

H. We have to stop the tuition increase. The next thing you know, they'll be charging $40,000 a semester.

I. Bill Clinton has no experience of serving in the military. To have Bill Clinton become President, and thus commander-in-chief of the armed forces of the United States, is like electing some passer-by on the street to fly the space shuttle.

Card 4

J. Everybody around me is using Darlie toothpaste, so I'm going to use it, too.

K. He was robbed while his neighbors were safe, because his room number was 1413.

L. If the child were allowed 40 minutes every day for computer games, he would get addicted to it. And then he would be likely to spend all his time surfing the net and neglect his studies entirely, and then he would be under evil influence of the Internet. Finally he would completely go astray. So in the first place the child must be strictly kept away from any computer games.

Logical fallacies:

A. Bandwagon
B. Invalid analogy
C. Red herring
D. False cause
E. Red herring
F. Ad hominem
G. Hasty generalization
H. Slippery slope
I. Invalid analogy
J. Bandwagon
K. False cause
L. Slippery slope

PPT/Directions	活动过程描述
2. *Directions:* Now we're going to have a group discussion on logical fallacies, that is, errors of reasoning. Each group will receive a card on which three examples of reasoning are given. You will discuss about them, and make judgment upon whether there are any loopholes in them and then describe them.	1. 将全班分为小组，每个小组包括四至六位学生，以便有效讨论。 2. 向学生说明本活动的主要内容为寻找逻辑漏洞，并将事先准备好的卡片分给小组（参见 Materials/Preparation）。每个小组领取一张卡片；如果多于四个小组，则有的小组可能领取到同样内容的卡片。
3. *Directions:* You'll have eight minutes to discuss about each card. You need to do the following: 1) Interpret the reasoning in each item; 2) Discuss whether there is a loophole in the conclusion and what's wrong with the reasoning if there is; 3) And write down the type of fallacy if anyone knows its name.	3. 告诉学生，小组讨论应在八分钟内完成以下步骤：第一，逐项阅读三项推理陈述；第二，讨论该推理是否存在漏洞？有什么问题？第三，是否有人知道该逻辑谬误的名称？ （布置任务、分发卡片，两至三分钟。）
4. **Notes** • Reasoning involved: _____ • Fallacy or not? _____ • Problem: _____ • Type of fallacy: _____	4. 学生讨论过程中需完成笔记，笔记框架（如左侧幻类片所示）应展示于PPT幻灯片上，以作参考。笔记可作为之后两分钟小组汇报的提纲。 （小组讨论不超过八分钟。）
6. A. All my classmates are preparing for study abroad. I must sign up for a TOEFL class too this weekend.	5. 八分钟后，请每个小组派代表上讲台，向全班汇报讨论结果。教师事先将四张卡片上的12条语料（A–L）分别放在12张幻灯片上，以备学生口头报告时使用。 6. 以Card 1为例，汇报程序为：1）朗读卡片上的推理案例A（如左侧幻灯片所示），以便让其他同学先了解语料内容；2）根据笔记框架，陈述本小组对该项推理案例的评价。不强求学生报出谬误的名称，重点在描述其内容。 7. 逐一完成案例B和C。载有B与C的文字内容的幻灯片应逐个播放。 8. 教师可给予简单评价或讲解，或对作为听众的同学进行启发式、引导式提问，目的是让学生明白案例中所反映的逻辑问题。 （将每个小组的陈述及班级讨论的时间控制在四分钟之内，其中陈述一般不超过两分钟。） 9. 各小组按此模式逐一完成口头汇报。

（待续）

PPT/Directions	活动过程描述
10-1 False Cause Event A happened. Event B happened after A. Therefore, A caused B. Fallacy: No connection between A and B.	10. 教师进行总结性陈述，尽可能将每一种逻辑谬误的主要特点描述清楚。 （总结部分约占五分钟。）
10-2 Hasty Generalization Specific Case(s) ⟶ General Rule Generalization	
10-3 Invalid Analogy Penguins are black and white. Some old TV shows are black and white. So, penguins are old TV shows.	
10-4 Red Herring We can't worry about the environment. We're in the middle of a war.	
10-5 Ad Hominem Your argument is wrong because you are so ugly and stinky!	
10-6 Bandwagon Everybody's Doing It!	
10-7 Slippery Slope A → B B → C … F → G Thus, A → G	

1. Reasoning is a very important part of "Methods of Persuasion" and consequently an essential component in persuasive speeches. This part is especially important for Chinese students, most of whom have not received systematic instruction on rhetoric. Out of this consideration, this activity may fill up almost the total duration of a 40-minute class period.

2. Of course, any briefer version of the activity may also be adopted. For example, seven examples corresponding to the seven fallacies may be given to the whole class for discussion, in which case the duration of the activity may be 10–15 minutes. This can also be used for a revision session or as a test.

3. The activity applies to various class sizes. If there are more than five groups (e.g., in a large class of more than 70 students), the instructor may invite only four groups to speak on the four cards respectively. To have a good time control but encourage participation, the instructor may invite comments from other groups who have discussed the same topics.

4. It is more important to remember the content of the fallacies than the names. Students should be encouraged to anatomize the loose logic rather than just resorting to the names of the fallacies.

5. The instructor should encourage independent thinking by allowing students to even defend the cases provided, for example, from the perspective of the audience's psychology. Why do speakers deliberately employ such logical fallacies? Why do people tend to believe them?

6. Try to link this unit to Unit 12 Critical Thinking.

Speeches for Special Occasions

UNDERSTANDING TEACHING

Teaching is the highest form of understanding.

—Aristotle

So what does a good instructor do? Create tension, but just the right amount.

—Donald Norman

There are two things that are more difficult than making an after-dinner speech: climbing a wall which is leaning toward you and kissing a girl who is leaning away from you.

—Winston Churchill

TEACHER'S GUIDE (Q & A)

➤ **特殊场合演讲包括哪些？**

- 特殊场合演讲从演讲场合来划分，主要包括介绍致辞（speeches of introduction）、颁奖致辞（speeches of presentation）、获奖致辞（speeches of acceptance）、祝酒辞（toasts）、纪念性演讲（commemorative speeches）。

- 特殊场合演讲可能是信息性的（如介绍致辞）、娱乐性的（如餐后演讲）、说服性加信息性的（如纪念性演讲），以及其他多重交流目的的（如某些场合下较长的祝酒辞等）。

➤ **该教学环节何时进行？**

- 在《演讲的艺术》第十版（中国版）教材中，该环节安排在第十五章"特殊场合演讲"(Speaking on Special Occasions, *APS*, Chapter 15, pp. 222–232)。本单元常自成一章，与其他章节关联不大。

- 在教学时间紧张的情况下，这一章节可能被忽略。但是在真实的工作和生活场景中，特殊场合演讲却很常见，因此建议不要删减这部分内容。

➤ **该环节的主要教学目标是什么？**

- 帮助学生了解和掌握特殊场合演讲的主要类型及其特点。

- 引导学生欣赏和学习经典的特殊场合演讲实例。
- 引导学生进行相关的演讲实践。

➤ 特殊场合演讲类型的主要特点是什么?

- 介绍致辞。用于向听众介绍主要演讲者或发言人。应注意遵守以下原则:
  A. 力求简洁（一般在两至三分钟）;
  B. 确保所传达的信息准确无误（特别注意被引见人姓名发音的准确及相关信息的准确）;
  C. 顺应说话的场合（例如正式与非正式场合、文化因素的考虑等）;
  D. 顺应被引见者的特点（例如不要过分夸张、避免涉及令人尴尬的生活细节等）;
  E. 顺应听众的特点（例如需要迎合听众的兴趣）。
- 颁奖致辞。用于颁发礼品、嘉奖或其他形式的公众认可等的场合,一般较为简短（一两分钟至五六分钟）。应注意遵守以下原则:
  A. 清楚地陈述获奖理由,概括获奖者与奖项相关的贡献或成就;
  B. 当听众对奖项不够熟悉时,简单介绍奖项内容;
  C. 同时需要关注和尊重未能获奖的参与者。
- 获奖致辞。主要目的是感谢,感谢给予奖项的人,感谢给予帮助的人。
- 祝酒辞。一般较简短,可以为几句话,用于表达欢迎或祝福身体健康或事业有成等。但在不同场合需要注意:
  A. 无论什么场合,真诚与热情都是第一原则,要营造融洽的气氛;
  B. 如遇到跨文化的场景,演讲者应事先熟悉相关语言表达;
  C. 在祝酒辞结尾处,举起酒杯,与肩持平,与对方保持目光接触,然后再饮杯中酒。
- 纪念性演讲。适用于颂扬、庆祝的场合,也包括悼词、节日祝词、献词等。演讲成功与否取决于演讲者是否能使用语言表达与演讲场合相应的思想与情感,因此修辞手法的运用至关重要。

➤ 常见的教学困难

- 教学时间有限,这部分往往因为没有时间处理而被舍弃。
- 许多特殊场合演讲对语言使用的要求极高,需要用语气来营造气氛,特别是纪念性演讲。因此师生可能选择放弃,或仅仅停留在欣赏的层次。
- 在介绍致辞、颁奖致辞、祝酒辞的演讲实践中,可能出现一味地追求娱乐效果,而不能实现场合所要求的更重要的目的。

20.1 Introducing the Speaker

Goal:	To give students an opportunity to practice a speech of introduction.
Class Size:	40 students.
Time:	30 mins.
Pre-Class Reading Assignment:	Speeches of Introduction (*APS*, Chapter 15, pp. 223–225).
Materials/Preparation:	A. A topic card.

Topic Card

Directions: Introduce a person (classmate, an expert or other celebrity) who is going to give a (keynote) speech on a big occasion. Your speech should be limited within two minutes.

Note: It is your responsibility to define the occasion.

B. Three types of speeches of introduction. (For the instructor's reference. This activity addresses Type C.)

Three Types of Speeches of Introduction

According to the length of the speech:

A. Speaker: a two-minute speech.
   Introducer: the speaker's name and one piece of information.
   E.g., Please help me welcome Kelley Mitchell from Lynnwood, Washington.

B. Speaker: a four- to five-minute speech.
   Introducer: the speaker's name and about two pieces of information on the speaker's background.
   E.g., Our next speaker is a fine arts major from Vancouver, British Columbia. Molly has been making clay sculptures and wheel-thrown pottery for 10 years. Today she has brought her potter's wheel to class to show us six steps to making a pot. Help me welcome Molly Wong.

C. Speaker: a longer speech.
   (See Materials/Preparation C.)

C.   Steps of introducing a guest speaker.

Steps of Introducing a Guest Speaker

Step 1: Briefly mention the topic but skip expressing an opinion on the speaker's view;

Step 2: Explain why the audience will be interested in the topic;

Step 3: Describe some personal information on the speaker as well as his or her credentials;

Step 4: Announce the speaker's name;

Step 5: Stay up front while the speaker moves from being seated to center stage.

Notes:

- Keep it brief, simple and clear.
- Avoid half-baked humor.
- Don't exaggerate the speaker's credentials.
- Say something new if the speaker is well-known.

In-Class Procedure

PPT/Directions	活动过程描述
1–2 Mini Lecture Three Types of Speeches of Introduction	1. 教师针对介绍致辞这一演讲类型进行简单讲解。参照 Materials/Preparation B，循序渐进。 2. 前两种类型介绍完毕，给每个小组一至两分钟时间，实践一下。之后，可邀请一两位学生在全班分享他们的演讲。教师应注意学生是否提供了准确的信息。 （五分钟。）
3–4 Prepare Your Speech • Who? Where? What? • What elements to include? • What sequence to follow? …	3. 将任务单（参见 Materials/Preparation A）及嘉宾介绍致辞步骤（Materials/Preparation C）分发给各组。提示材料A中的要求以及材料C中的注意事项。 4. 学生分小组（每组最好不超过四人）进行准备，每小组准备一个演讲即可。提醒学生：不一定必须遵循所建议的步骤。 （小组准备七分钟。）

（待续）

PPT/Directions	活动过程描述
5. Presentation and Evaluation · Basic information covered? · Language proper? · Presentation clear?	5. 邀请四至五组上台演讲，其他小组进行点评。点评小组需要审视以下几个方面：第一，必要的内容是否均已涉及？第二，语言使用是否得体？第三，口头陈述是否清楚？ 教师适时给予引导。
6. Note In reality, research is often the first thing to do!	6. 提醒学生，在真实情景下准备此类演讲，研究工作不可少。需上网或通过其他途径查阅发言人的个人信息。 7. 可以选择其中一个演讲，重点讲评，并要求小组课后查阅资料，重新整理完成讲稿写作。

Comments/Reflections

1. If students find it more interesting to introduce a classmate, the instructor may match a speaker with an introducer instead of arranging group discussions. In this case, the introducer needs to interview the speaker in order to acquire necessary information. It is important to note that when the speaker is someone familiar to the audience, the introducer should bring new information which inspires the audience.

2. Again, remind students that research is always the most important thing to do when preparing for a formal occasion.

本活动的设计基于以下文献来源：Sikes, Shirley. (1995). Introducing the Speaker. In Lucas, Stephen E. (ed.) *Selections from the Speech Communication Teacher, 1991–1994*. Madison, Wisconsin: McGraw-Hill. 59–60.

Goal: To introduce students to the art of paying tribute to a person that has been pivotal in their lives, have them practice positive interpersonal skills, and demonstrate the importance of pathos in a credible speech.

Class Size: 40 students.

Time: 10 mins. + assignments + 30 mins.

Pre-Class Reading Assignment: Speaking on Special Occasions (*APS*, Chapter 15, pp. 222–232).

Materials/Preparation: None.

In-Class Procedure

PPT/Directions	活动过程描述
The First Class Meeting	**第一次课**
1–2 Why is it easier to criticize than compliment? What constitutes an "admirable" person?	1. 这个活动的主要目的是让学生学会"颂扬"别人的演讲。 2. 前一次课结束之前，组织学生讨论以下问题： A. 为什么人们总是喜欢批评别人而不是赞扬别人？ B. "令人敬佩（admirable）的人"拥有哪些品质？ （五分钟。） 3. 在分享学生的讨论结果的同时，提醒学生：大部分人没有受过"赞扬别人"的训练。这正是这次活动的主题。
Assignment	**布置任务**
4. Who's your hero? An interview: How much do you know about your hero? Pathos: Appeal to the audience's emotion.	4. 布置任务：下次课上要求学生进行两分钟的颂扬演讲。学生需要做三项准备： A. 选定一位熟悉的人，可以是过世的或在世的。建议选择父母、老师、同学、朋友，以及给自己影响较大的人。 B. 需要进行采访。采访对象可以是颂扬对象，也可以是熟悉颂扬对象的人。提醒学生采访环节不可省略，而且应该集中采访一两个问题。 C. 需要完成一份详细提纲或讲稿。 向学生介绍"情感诉求"，提醒学生本次演讲需要在情感上打动听众。 （五分钟。）

（待续）

PPT/Directions	活动过程描述
The Second Class Meeting	**第二次课**
5. Presentations Who's the best eulogy speaker of the class? • Ethos • Pathos • Logos	5. 第二次课的口头陈述分为两个阶段： A. 学生先在小组中演讲。40人的班级可分为六至八个小组。评选出小组最佳演讲。 B. 各组的最佳演讲在全班再进行一次，评选出班级最佳演讲。 提醒学生关注三方面的标准：伦理诉求，即演讲者自身所表现出的可信度；情感诉求，即是否真实、感人；逻辑诉求，即内容是否中心突出，有理有据。 教师对学生演讲进行点评与分析。 （30—35分钟。）

Comments/Reflections

1. We often observe that people are much quicker to criticize and insult others than to offer praise or compliments. This activity is created, in addition to learning this specific type of public speech, to show students the benefits that can accompany complimentary behavior. Similarly, the activity combines positive interpersonal skills with public speaking skills.

2. It should be noted that the interview conducted as part of the activity calls on a variety of skills: Students must draw on interpersonal skills that will facilitate an interview that results in useful information for the speech; and they must think quickly during the interview to build on the desired information.

3. A predictable problem found among students is that they tend to throw scattered information about the person to the audience. So it is important to tell students to focus on one or several qualities in the interview and the drafting of the speech. Biographical information, examples or particular accomplishments, and opinions of others provide supporting evidence of why the person is worthy of the audience's praise and/or admiration.

4. It is expected that students develop the art of praise as a method of communication. In addition, the class will develop a deeper appreciation of the people around them.

5. Having reflected on the "heroes" that influenced them, and having come to appreciate what it is about these people that is worthy of praise, students are more conscious of respecting others for their own unique qualities and accomplishments.

本活动的设计基于以下文献来源：Lamansky, Martin. (1995). Getting to Know My Hero: The Speech of Tribute. In Lucas, Stephen E. (ed.) *Selections from the Speech Communication Teacher, 1991–1994*. Madison, Wisconsin: McGraw-Hill. 58–59.

Goal:	To equip students with a format for the construction of eulogy and learn how to appreciate a eulogy.
Class Size:	Any.
Time:	40 mins.
Pre-Class Reading Assignment:	Speaking on Special Occasions (*APS*, Chapter 15, pp. 222–232).
Materials/Preparation:	A. Methods of arrangement for eulogies.

Methods of Arrangement for Eulogies

I. Introduction
   1. Acknowledgment of the occasion
   2. Acknowledgment of the family
      a. Immediate family
      b. Other appropriate relatives
      c. Friends and community members

II. Body
   1. Memory
      a. Personal memories of the speaker
      b. Memories of the family
      c. Public accomplishments or contributions of the deceased to the community and their profession
   2. Consolation (comments of the deceased about others)
      a. Comments about the family
      b. Comments about the friends and community members
   3. The official record

III. Conclusion (inspiration from the life of the deceased)

B. Eulogy for Princess Diana given by her brother Charles Spencer (both the video and the script, available on heep. unipus. cn).

PPT/Directions	活动过程描述
Pre-Class Assignment	**课前任务**
1. Video: Eulogy for Princess Diana by Earl Charles Spencer · Introduction · Body · Conclusion	1. 给学生分发查尔斯·斯宾塞伯爵在英国王储戴安娜王妃葬礼上的悼词。要求学生认真阅读，并查阅关于戴安娜与其弟斯宾塞伯爵的相关资料。此外，观看演讲视频。 学生下次上课前必须熟悉讲稿的内容，否则将会影响教学进程。 请学生关注这个葬礼演讲的基本结构：开头、主体、结尾。
In-Class Procedure	**课堂活动过程描述**
2. Watch the video.	2. 与学生一起观看演讲视频。（八分钟。） 3. 微型讲座。向学生讲解悼词的一般组成要素及结构（参见 Materials/Preparation A）。
4. Group discussion. I. Introduction 　1. The occasion 　2. The family II. Body 　1. Memory 　　a. Personal memories 　　b. Memories of the family 　　c. Contributions 　2. Consolation (comments of the deceased about others) 　3. The official record III. Conclusion	4. 小组讨论。 给每个小组发一份 Method of Arrangement for Eulogies 复印件。让学生对照戴安娜王妃葬礼演讲的文字稿，找出结构框架中各项的相应内容。 提醒学生，这份悼词与普通人的悼词不完全相同，并非严格遵循所提供的悼词结构原则，学生只要能找出基本对应的部分即可。（例如，The official record 一项可能是空缺的，但是可以让学生思考这一项为什么空缺。） 提醒学生关注演讲人使用语言营造的气氛。 （若为节约课堂时间，也可采用将不同的部分分配给不同小组的方式。） （10分钟。）
5. The best English eulogy!	5. 小组讨论结束后，由教师引导，进行全班讨论。教师适时地给予提示和帮助。 6. 鼓励学生课后模仿演讲视频，学习语言。

1. In public speaking texts, eulogies are usually mentioned as a special occasion speech or type of commemorative speech. In fact, eulogies are usually offered at funeral memorial services both in Western countries and in China. Understanding the English eulogy helps students understand the Western culture.

2. This activity acquaints students with a basic structure of a eulogy and provides students with an opportunity to appreciate perhaps the most famous eulogy in British history.

3. Students may need substantial assistance from the instructor in the analysis of Princess Diana's eulogy given by his bother Earl Charles Spencer, as the background is not familiar to many of today's students and that the language is of a quite formal style.

4. This sample eulogy also provides an excellent example of the use of language in terms of both extensive and precise use of vocabulary and rhetorical devices. It provides good pronunciation material too for students to imitate.

本活动的设计基于以下文献来源：Cates, Carl. (1998). Eulogies as a Special Occasion Speech. In Lucas, Stephen E. (ed.) *Selections from the Speech Communication Teacher, 1994–1996.* Madison, Wisconsin: McGraw-Hill. 85–86.

Impromptu Speeches

UNDERSTANDING TEACHING

It usually takes me more than three weeks to prepare a good impromptu speech.

—Mark Twain

Those who would teach public speaking by indiscriminately handling out topics for impromptu speeches render a disservice to an ancient and honorable art; they simply teach the art of mouthing nothing—a practice which violates the basic purpose of speechmaking: the communication of ideas. Public speaking must never be mere glibness empty of thought and ideas.

—Bert Bradley

The best way to learn is to do; the worst way to teach is to talk.

—Paul Halmos

TEACHER'S GUIDE (Q & A)

➤ **什么是即兴演讲?**

- 即兴演讲是针对有备演讲（prepared speech）而言的。前者的准备时间极短，甚至没有，因此不会提前写讲稿；后者通常有较长时间准备，且多数情况下完成了讲稿写作。
- 严格地讲，即兴演讲是指几乎无准备的，或只有很短准备时间（如一两分钟或两三分钟）的演讲。如许多竞选演讲、竞聘演讲中有当场给题目的即兴演讲环节。
- 我们平时所说的即兴演讲，如演讲大赛中的即兴演讲部分，或课堂上即兴完成的演讲任务，更像半即兴演讲或半脱稿演讲（extemporaneous speech），因为演讲者通常有数分钟甚至更长的准备时间，此外还可以记简单的笔记。往往选手演讲时也可以参照笔记。本单元所说的即兴演讲包括即兴演讲和半即兴演讲。

➤ **该教学环节何时进行?**

- 《演讲的艺术》第十版（中国版）教材中，集中讲授即兴演讲或半即兴演讲的章节包括：

   A. Speaking Extemporaneously (*APS*, Chapter 3, pp. 36–37);

B. Speaking Impromptu, Speaking Extemporaneously (*APS*, Chapter 11, pp. 148–149);

C. Impromptu Speech (*APS*, Chapter 16, pp. 239–243).

- 除了演讲准备这个维度以外，即兴演讲和有备演讲从内容、组织、语言、甚至演讲表达方面，几乎无异。因此该单元的活动同样适用于 *APS* 教材中的大部分章节。

➤ **即兴演讲有什么技巧？**

如果即兴演讲有技巧可言，也不会脱离公众演讲的基本原则。但要在几秒钟到几分钟的准备时间内完成较为满意的演讲，一些策略可能有所帮助。

- 首先要克服"乱"，即要讲清楚。即使在无时间准备的情况下，遵循一些通用的基本组织方式，也可大大提高演讲的清晰度和演讲者的自信。例如：

  A. PREP，即 Point—Reason—Example—Point。核心观点是什么？什么理由？能否举例说明？最后再总结和强调一下观点。

  B. 5W，即"谁（Who）？""什么（What）？""什么时间（When）？""什么地点（Where）？""为什么（Why）？"

  C. Issue—Pros vs. Cons—My View。出现了什么问题？有何不同见解？我的见解？

  D. Past—Present—Future。

- 中心观点一定要明确。
- 观察角度要新，但一定要有支撑细节（supporting details）。
- 在支撑细节不足时，使用自己或周围人的经历。
- 即兴演讲中的幽默更加真实，效果也更好。
- 如果时间允许，尽量将开头和结尾的语言组织好。
- 演讲时，语速可放慢一些，以保证思维的流畅。
- 记住：听众的信心完全来自演讲者。
- 演讲时，尽可能增加与听众的互动，让演讲直接指向听众。

➤ **教与学的误区**

- 即兴演讲才能反映一个人真正的演讲水平，因此，演讲教学的重点应该放在即兴演讲训练上。
- 即兴演讲就是没有准备时间，所以，只有每次演讲实践中取消准备时间，演讲能力才能提高。
- 要想在演讲比赛的即兴演讲环节取胜，最重要的是能展示新奇的观点，和别人的观点差异越大越好，即出奇制胜。

➤ **如何提高即兴演讲能力？**

- 即兴演讲的技巧或许能帮助初学者得到更好的发挥，但真正提高即兴演讲能力，其功夫主要在平时。
- 从某种角度说，有备演讲也是即兴演讲的前期准备。即兴演讲不需要写演讲稿，但是对于初学者而言，写作演讲稿、写好演讲稿是必经的修炼过程。
- 真正做到即兴现场发挥得好，需要先经过有备演讲的训练过程。其中最重要的两个方面是知识储备和思维训练。知识储备来自广泛阅读和丰富经历，即我们常说的间接经验和直接经验；思维习惯的培养主要针对思维的清晰和严谨以及创新和创意思维（详见 Unit 12 Critical Thinking）。

21.1 Speaking Impromptu: Challenge Your Courage and Knowledge

Goal: To help students improve the quality of ideas and organization in an impromptu speech exercise, and to provide a climate which encourages listening, speaking, critical thinking, and creative thinking.

Class Size: Ideally less than 40 students.

Time: 20 mins.

Pre-Class Reading Assignment: None.

Materials/Preparation: Two topic cards. (A number of spare copies may be needed for group discussion.)

Topic Card 1

1. My ideal kind of job.
2. Explain how to make… (e.g., a meal, a thing…)
3. Three changes I'd like to make to my university curriculum.
4. Weakness of attitude becomes weakness of character. —Albert Einstein

Topic Card 2

1. How to save money.
2. Happiness.
3. Our university should…
4. Perfection of means and confusion of ends seem to characterize our age. —Albert Einstein

Sample materials for later use if the activity is to be repeated:

Scenario 1

Some people believe that part of the success of McDonald's has come from the company's willingness to cater to local tastes, as what it has done in China over the years. However, others argue that it is very dangerous for the company to continue to do so because it will finally lose its charm completely if the raw material, ingredients and cooking methods are changed. Suppose you are the CEO of McDonald's (China), how would you respond? Should food maintain its original taste or cater to local tastes?

Scenario 2

Exchange students from Northwest University of the US, who arrived at your university just two days ago, will study here in the coming six months. They've been given a general orientation about life and study here; however, they'd like to know more about the city—transportation, shops and other attractions. Please give them a speech on what they are interested in and help make their life here more convenient and rewarding.

🕐 In-Class Procedure

PPT/Directions	活动过程描述
1–2 *Directions:* Two students will speak impromptu on one of four given topics. The speakers will have eight minutes to prepare and two minutes to speak. And then, they need to respond to a number of questions or comments from different groups. Guidelines for Speakers Preparation (eight mins.) ↓ Speech (two mins.) ↓ Q & A (two mins.)	1. 需要两位学生进行两分钟的即兴演讲。两位学生可以是自愿的，或随机挑选的，或由小组推选产生。可遵循教师上课的习惯。 2. 两位学生分别领取Topic Card 1和Topic Card 2（参见Materials/Preparation）中的一张任务单，从四个题目中选择其中一个进行即兴演讲，演讲时间为两分钟，准备时间为八分钟。这两位学生需要到教室外面准备。演讲顺序应在此时已确定。 演讲学生应提前知道演讲的程序（如左侧幻灯片所示），两分钟演讲之后，需要回答各组所提的问题，每个问题的回答时间不超过30秒钟。
3–4 Guidelines for Audience/Judges I. Definition of the topic • Clear? • Pertinent? • Unique? Insightful? Interesting? II. Organization, language and delivery • Clear? Logical? Coherent? • Proper style? • Enunciation? Volume? Eye contact? Facial expression? III. Suggestions for improvement • Improvable? How? • Need to change a topic?	3. 期间，各小组同步讨论所分配的即兴演讲题目。将两张任务单中所含八个题目分配给小组。以四个小组为例，每个小组分配两题。将相应的任务单分发给小组。 4. 小组讨论的主要任务是准备演讲之后的提问或点评，因此讨论过程也是学习评估演讲的方法。讨论的线索可分为三个部分。 第一，对题目本身的解读（内容）。 A. 演讲人对题目中关键概念的解读是否清楚？是否和你的有差异？ B. 演讲是否有独到的见解和视角？是否有新意？

（待续）

PPT/Directions	活动过程描述
Tips for Questions & Comments • Be concrete. • Be constructive.	第二，对演讲的评估（组织、语言与演讲表达）。 A. 演讲的逻辑和语言表达是否够清楚？你是否全部理解了？ B. 演讲是否有明确的中心？ C. 口齿、音量、视线交流、手势如何？ 第三，改进措施。 A. 哪些细节问题可以改善？通过什么样的方式进行改善？ B. 哪些问题关乎全局，需要整体修改或放弃重来？
5–7 **Q & A**	5. 准备时间结束，准备演讲。指定两位学生分别对下面的Q & A环节进行记录。 6. 邀请第一位学生进行演讲。计时。 7. 负责这个题目的小组进行提问或点评，之后鼓励其他小组即兴提问。提问或点评应不少于五个，演讲人需逐一回应。教师作为活动的主持人，将总时间控制在两分钟左右，并在需要时给予提示。 8. 邀请第二位学生进行演讲。程序同上。
9–10 **Summary**	9. 请做记录的两位同学进行Q & A环节的总结发言。将时间控制在每人一分钟到一分半钟。 10. 教师总结。鼓励演讲的学生在课后对演讲进行反思，并在此基础上完成一篇演讲稿或一份详细的演讲提纲。

Comments/Reflections

1. Though impromptu speeches are challenging, students often get excited about them. The excitement often comes out of curiosity to see how others could handle those difficult situations especially when the topic is hard to grasp. However, if classroom activities are so designed only for students to satisfy their curiosity, they won't learn much and their interest gradually wanes. This is something instructors should always bear in mind.

2. The key to this activity is to hold all students' interest and meanwhile make sure that they are engaged and learn. This is why in this activity, the spotlight moves from the speakers to the majority of students. Almost everybody has an important task to complete. The speakers are the focus of attention yet the audience are judges, question masters, and commentators. What a fun! But they really learn when properly guided.

3. The activity may be adapted to different purposes and situations. Whatever changes are made, make sure that students have something to say, can fill up the speaking time, and are stimulated to think based on yet beyond their range of knowledge. Here are some suggestions:

A. Try to limit the impromptu speaking time to one minute if students are absolutely novice public speakers or when their English ability is not enough for them to speak continuously. Offer facilitation as to the organization and the idea if needed. Don't leave students as they are. Help them succeed!

B. Make the tasks for both the speakers and the audience more challenging toward the end of the semester when they've made considerable progress. For example, extend the speaking time up to three minutes (but not more than that), ask the audience to make a short but well organized comment of, say, 40 seconds or one minute, etc.

C. Use more interesting topics instead.

21.2   Which Department Can Win the Fund?

Goal:	To practice impromptu speeches on campus-related topics in a unique, competitive yet friendly atmosphere.
Class Size:	25–40 students.
Time:	35 mins.
Pre-Class Reading Assignment:	None; or any of the following sections:

A. Speaking to Persuade (*APS*, Chapter 14, pp. 192–221);
B. Speaking Impromptu, Speaking Extemporaneously (*APS*, Chapter 11, pp. 148–149);
C. Impromptu Speech (*APS*, Chapter 16, pp. 239–243).

Materials/Preparation:
A. An award (a certificate, a book...) for the winning group.
B. Four envelops, each of which contains a piece of paper with the name of one of four departments—Finance & Economics, Music, Education and Computer Technology on it, and the sequence order of speaking.
C. Five copies of the evaluation form.

Department	Idea (10)	Delivery (10)	Teamwork (10)	Q & A (20)	Total
Finance & Economics					
Music					
Education					
Computer Technology					

PPT/Directions	活动过程描述
1–3 *Directions:* In order to encourage teaching and learning, the University Board decides to offer a 30,000 *yuan* grant to one of the four departments—Finance & Economics, Music, Education and Computer Technology. Today the four departments are going to bid for the grant. Groups A, B, C and D each will make a four-minute bid presentation, each representing a department, to the University Board consisting of five judges randomly chosen from the class. The winning group will receive an award.	1. 将学生分为四个小组。 2. 介绍此次活动的任务：来自一所大学的四个不同系科要竞争学校的一笔发展基金。四个小组将分别代表四个系科，每组各进行四分钟的竞标演说，讲述该系为何需要这笔基金，申请到了经费之后打算如何使用。 3. 全体学生中随机挑选五名学生（或自愿报名）组成校董事会，担任评委工作，该评委不代表任何系科，将仅就发言者的演讲进行评判。
4. Finance & Economics Computer Technology Music Education	4. 每组派代表到讲台前抽取一个装有系科名称的信封，信封里还有发言序号。各组不得向其他小组公开自己的系科以及发言序号。
5. Discussion ↓ Presentation ↓ Q & A ↓ Comments from the Board ↓ Awards	5. 向全班同学展示活动的步骤，即小组讨论—即兴竞标演讲—评委提问—评委点评—颁奖。如左侧幻灯片所示。 演讲环节中，小组可派代表，也可集体演说。集体演说在评分上会有额外加分。 PPT上向全班展示评分表。

6.
 	
Prompts for Discussion
 	
1. Why?
   Your strength or urgent need?
2. What?
   Plan?
3. How?
   Benefits to students and university?
	6. 各组进行讨论，准备竞标演讲。讨论内容包括两方面：一，申请基金的理由；二，未来的发展方案。小组还需准备在陈述之后裁判提出的一个提问，回答时间不超过一分钟。讨论线索可参照如左侧幻灯片的提示，也可由小组自行决定。要求小组记笔记。（讨论环节控制在五至六分钟。）
	
	7. 将评分表发给五位校董会评委。校董会在小组讨论同时，商议评分规则，以及稍后提问和点评环节。

（待续）

PPT/Directions	活动过程描述
8. Speech Procedure 1. Presentation (up to four mins.) 2. Q & A (up to one min.)	8. 准备时间到，小组按照发言序号。每组发言时间不得超过四分钟。之后回答评委团的一个问题，回答时间不超过一分钟。（每个小组的总时间不超过五分半钟。）
9–11 Comments Awards	9. 四个小组分别完成任务。评委团打分、算分。期间，教师可先邀请同学进行即兴评论。 10. 评委团中一位代表宣布结果并简要点评，其他四人可针对一组给出点评。教师也可补充点评。 11. 颁奖。

Comments/Reflections

1. This activity has been adopted in my class more than once and turned out to be well received by students. The form of extemporaneous speech and competition add to its attraction. More importantly, students gave much better performance in terms of linguistic output—both in content and in the range of vocabulary and the complexity of sentence structure.

2. The activity works especially well with small classes of 25–40 students where everybody is involved and most of them have a chance to speak in class. The role of judge is challenging yet attractive as the judges who assume full authority have to make endeavors to live up to the title. Other students immensely enjoy presenting why they are more eligible than others for the grant.

3. It may apply to big classes too if time allows, in which case more departments may come in and the speaking time may be shortened.

4. The biggest challenge here is to make sure that students have something to say. In consideration of this, the instructor should carefully choose the departments which can't be too unfamiliar to students. Or, alternatively the instructor may provide some information about the departments. He or she may even provide reading materials if needed. Sometimes the instructor may find that further facilitation is absolutely necessary when language itself is a big issue. The key is to do everything necessary to ensure a smooth flow of the procedure.

5. The activity is used for impromptu speech training here, which means very limited preparation is allowed. However, an adapted version may encourage extensive reading and research prior to class, in which case some less familiar departments may come in and the task is assigned a week in advance. And students will automatically have their information literacy (See Unit 11) enhanced as they have to decide what kind of information is needed and try to search, sort, evaluate and select what they need.

（供稿人：季璇 南京师范大学；改编人：田朝霞）

Goal: To provide students with an opportunity to practice impromptu speeches by making a public-interest ad promoting China's national image.

Class Size: Any.

Time: 30 mins.

Pre-Class Reading Assignment:
A. Speaking Impromptu, Speaking Extemporaneously (*APS*, Chapter 11, pp. 148–149);
B. Impromptu Speech (*APS*, Chapter 16, pp. 239–243).

Materials/Preparation:
A. A video clip: "China's National Image—Figure" (available on heep. unipus. cn).
B. Four-step method: Making an impromptu speech.

Four-Step Method: Making an Impromptu Speech

Step 1: State the point you are answering.

Step 2: State the point you wish to make.

Step 3: Support your point with evidence and reasoning.

Step 4: Summarize your point.

C. Major figures of speech.

A List of Major Figures of Speech

- Metaphor (隐喻、暗喻)
- Simile (明喻)
- Parallelism (排比)
- Repetition (重复、反复)
- Alliteration (头韵)
- Antithesis (对偶)

D. Students' sample speech.

To Promote China's National Image in the World: Yao Ming

[样例：“姚明”的演讲稿——中国国家形象宣传片]

【*music: 一段手机音乐响起*】 【*Make a pose: 手握篮球投篮姿势*】

Hello, everyone!

Do you know who I am?

Yes, of course you do.

Yes, you may guess right from my height.

I am Yao Ming, the famous basketball player from China.

Representing all the Chinese athletes, I want the world to hear my voice:

When people doubt that Chinese people are not able to play basketball well,

I prove that a Chinese player can become a member in the NBA league.

When people doubt that I cannot have an outstanding performance in the NBA,

I prove that I am now one of the best basketball players in the world.

When people doubt that Chinese and Asian athletes cannot compete with Western athletes in sports, we prove that we are the most competitive team in the Olympic Games.

Yes, we are Chinese.

Yes, we are Chinese athletes.

Yes, we are good Chinese athletes.

And here we are.

Yes, we can!

Yes, we can!!

Yes, we can!!! 【*Make a pose: 双手上举张开, 展示自信。*】

【说明：本演讲稿是由路遥同学的课堂现场即兴之作, 后经过聂薇老师修改而成。】

PPT/Directions	活动过程描述
1–2 **Mini-Lecture** • Four-step method • Figures of speech	1. 微型讲座:"四步法"(参见 Materials/Preparation B)即兴演讲。 如果时间允许,也可以简单介绍有关即兴演讲的准备、注意事项及问答环节方面的知识。 2. 复习主要修辞手法(参见 Materials/Preparation C)。

3–5
 	
Video
"China's National Image—Figure"
 	
Impromptu Speech
• Four-step
• Figure of speech
	3. 播放视频前,对视频进行说明:"中国国家形象宣传片——人物篇",长度为一分钟;只有音乐,没有说话声音。
	
	4. 向学生交代任务:
	  A. 挑选并扮演视频中出现的或视频之外的一个人物,进行一分钟演讲;
	  B. 演讲目的为提升中国形象;
	  C. 必须遵循"四步法";
	  D. 必须使用一种修辞手法。
	  E. 准备三分钟。
	
	5. 播放视频。

6.
 	
Showcase
• Group or individual
• Pose & speech
	6. 事先将全班分为若干小组。准备完毕,各小组(可以是一位代表或全体)上台表演。为避免枯燥,并节约课堂时间,可以选择表演人数不超过12人。
	
	  A. 为活跃气氛,缓解紧张情绪,小组到教室前面需先集体亮相,根据主题内容集体摆出造型,之后,每个成员亦需摆姿势亮相。
	
	  B. 然后,逐一以某位名人的口吻进行英文即兴演讲。
	
	  C. 可使用手机进行音乐伴奏。形式可以灵活,活泼一点更好。

7.
 	
Peer Evaluation
 	
Instructor's Comments
• Organization
• Content
• Language
• Delivery skills
• Style
• Creativity
	7. 点评。
	  A. 第一组演讲结束后,下一组学生对该组学生表现进行点评,以此类推。
	
	  B. 每两三组展示之后,教师点评并提出改进建议。之后下一组进行演讲。以此类推。
	
	8. 最后,给学生展示样例——"姚明"的演讲稿(参见 Materials/Preparation D)。
	
	教师从组织(organization)、内容(content)、语言(language)、演讲表达(delivery)、台风(style)、创造性(creativity)等几个方面点评。先以鼓励评价为主,再提建设性的改进意见。

1. Tracking multiple goals, this activity is highly recommended to instructors who wish to integrate theories into practice and provide students with a pleasant atmosphere.

    First, it provides students with an opportunity to practice the four-step method of making an impromptu speech and figures of speech at the same time.

    Second, it creates a light and entertaining learning atmosphere with a group making poses together and speaking one by one. Students are very familiar with those Chinese elites in the video; therefore, it is not difficult for them to imitate their heroes.

    Third, it stimulates imagination and creativity, as well as improve language proficiency.

    Fourth, it helps enhance students' sense of national pride.

2. The instructor may be flexible in grouping the class according to its size. This activity applies to both group activity and individual performance. It is up to the instructor to decide which form to take. However, group activity usually works better for it creates a light and entertaining learning atmosphere in class and students will not feel nervous with group members performing together in front of the class. It is full of fun.

3. This activity works well for English learners at different levels.

    A. It can be used for beginning level learners who are less able to produce longer speeches on their own. If it is still difficult for beginners, the speech can be made in Chinese first, then in English.

    B. It can be used for intermediate and advanced level students who are encouraged to use creative thinking and produce more complicated language output.

4. After students finish their speeches, the instructor may comment on the strong points in students' performance with great encouragement followed by constructive criticism in terms of organization, content, language, delivery, style, and creativity.

（供稿人：聂薇 北京外国语大学；改编人：田朝霞）

图书在版编目（CIP）数据

演讲的艺术课堂活动教师手册 / 田朝霞，周红兵编著. — 北京 ：外语教学与研究出版社，2015.2（2025.4 重印）
（全国高等学校外语教师丛书. 课堂活动系列）
ISBN 978-7-5135-5611-8

Ⅰ. ①演… Ⅱ. ①田… ②周… Ⅲ. ①演讲－语言艺术－课堂教学－高等学校－教学参考资料－英、汉 Ⅳ. ①H019

中国版本图书馆 CIP 数据核字（2015）第 039650 号

出 版 人　王　芳
项目负责　陈　静
责任编辑　郑建萍　谭胜方
装帧设计　吴德胜
出版发行　外语教学与研究出版社
社　　址　北京市西三环北路 19 号（100089）
网　　址　https://www.fltrp.com
印　　刷　河北虎彩印刷有限公司
开　　本　889×1194　1/16
印　　张　13.25
版　　次　2015 年 5 月第 1 版 2025 年 4 月第 11 次印刷
书　　号　ISBN 978-7-5135-5611-8
定　　价　46.90 元

如有图书采购需求，图书内容或印刷装订等问题，侵权、盗版书籍等线索，请拨打以下电话或关注官方服务号：
客服电话：400 898 7008
官方服务号：微信搜索并关注公众号"外研社官方服务号"
外研社购书网址：https://fltrp.tmall.com

物料号：256110001

记载人类文明
沟通世界文化
www.fltrp.com